THE MYSTICAL POWER OF MUSIC

Rabbi Avraham Arieh Trugman

TARGUM PRESS

First published 2005
Copyright © 2005 by Avraham Arieh Trugman
ISBN 1-56871-346-0

All rights reserved

No part of this publication may be translated, reproduced, stored in a retrieval system, or transmitted in any form or by any means, electronic, mechanical, photocopying, recording, or otherwise, without prior permission in writing from both the copyright holder and the publisher.

Published by:
TARGUM PRESS, INC.
22700 W. Eleven Mile Rd.
Southfield, MI 48034
E-mail: targum@netvision.net.il
Fax: 888-298-9992
www.targum.com

Distributed by:
FELDHEIM PUBLISHERS
208 Airport Executive Park
Nanuet, NY 10954
www.feldheim.com

Printed in Israel

Rav Zev Leff

Rabbi of Moshav Mattityahu
Rosh Hayeshiva Yeshiva Gedola Matisyahu
D.N. Modi'in 71917 \Tel. (08) 976-1138 Fax (08) 976-5326

I have had the pleasure to read the manuscript of *The Mystical Power of Music* by my dear friend and colleague Rabbi Avraham Trugman. Rabbi Trugman has truly composed a symphony of ideas, presenting music from a Torah perspective. He first adeptly traces the sources in the written and oral Torah that point to the importance of music. He then draws upon many and varied Torah commentaries to explain rationally, scientifically, and esoterically the effect and impact that music has on the individual and on the world. The thoughts he expounds on *Perek Shirah*, the songs of the various creations, are especially well done.

I recommend this work as an interesting, informative, and inspiring presentation of music from a Torah perspective. May Hashem grant Rabbi Trugman long life and health to enable him to continue to serve *klal Yisroel* by contributing of his unique portion in Torah and service to Hashem Yisborach.

Sincerely,
With Torah blessings

[signature]

Rabbi Zev Leff

Rabbi Yitzchak Ginsburgh

Gal Einai Institute, P.O. Box 1015, Kfar Chabad 72915, Israel

Dear Avraham Arieh,

In the *Zohar* we are taught that Moshe Rabbeinu knew to sing all the songs of creation and the songs of all the souls of Israel. By the power of song he could even resurrect the dead.

In Hebrew, the numerical value of "the power of song" (כח השיר), is 543, the identical value of the Holy Name of God that God revealed to Moshe before the Exodus: "I shall be who I shall be" (אהיה אשר אהיה). (In "small numbering," "the power of song" equals 21 — "I shall be" (אהיה).) 543 is the mirror image of 345 — Moshe!

By the power of song we reveal our true identity, return to our soul root in God and merit the true and complete redemption with the coming of Moshiach, Amen.

Wishing you all the best and great success with your new book *The Mystical Power of Music*.

Yitzchak Ginsburgh

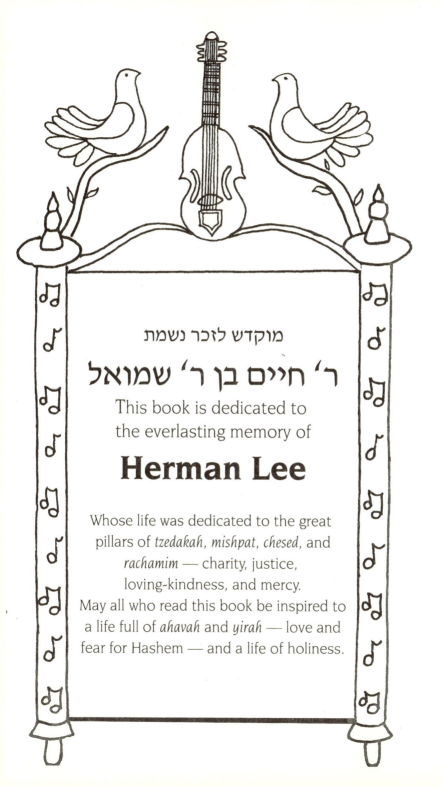

In loving memory of our teachers who taught us
that the study of Torah is a *mikvah*:
HaRav Shlomo ben HaRav Naftali and
HaRav Ben Tzion Chaim Shlomie Meshullam Zusia
ben Yaakov Yisrael

Henoch Dov, Sari, Ari, Yehoshua, and
Chanan Hoffman

We would like to thank
Rabbi Avraham Arieh and Rachel Trugman
for giving so much to our family, being our inspiration, and welcoming us into their home.
Hashem should continue to give you the strength
to encourage others and arouse the sparks within
each of us.

The Silverstones

Contents

Acknowledgments 11
Introduction 15

MUSIC IN THE JEWISH TRADITION. 19
    The Connection between Music and Divine Inspiration. . . 23
    Music Rooted in the Higher Spheres 25
    Music in the Temple 27
    The Ten Archetypal Songs. 32

MUSIC, SONG, AND PRAYER. 39
    Serving God through Prayer and Song 44
    Music and Prayer as Connection 46

TORAH AND THE SONG OF THE CREATOR 49
    The Inner Dynamics of Creation 55
    A Unified Universe. 58

THE SONG OF CREATION 61
    The Songs of *Perek Shirah* 66
    The Singers of *Perek Shirah* 68
    The Four Ascending Levels of Prayer 73
    The Connection to the Ten *Sefirot* 77

MUSIC AND SCIENCE 79
    Scientific Fact and the *Sefirot* 84
    String Theory 87
    Unity in the Forces of the Universe 89
    The Music of the Animal Kingdom 93
    The Music of the Vegetable Kingdom 96
    The Music of the Mineral Kingdom 101

FINDING ONE'S OWN SONG 105
    The Spark of God Within 109
    Each Person's Unique Mission 111
    Being in Tune with One's Mission 114
    Resonance with the World 115
    The Direct Connection to God 117
    How Do We Find Our Inner Song? 120
    Seeking Help through Prayer 122
    Reaching Our Song through Torah 124
    Meditation 126
    Nature 129
    Music on Every Level of Existence 131

    About the Author 134
    About Ohr Chadash 135

Acknowledgments

Recognizing the good others do for us and acknowledging them both privately and publicly is a very strong Jewish ethic. It is with this idea in mind that I undertake to thank those people who have helped make this book possible.

I begin with the wonderful staff at Targum Press: Thanks to Miriam Zakon for her input at the beginning and the end of the project; to Chaya Baila Gavant for her fine editorial skills and expertise, which helped greatly in fine-tuning the text; and to Diane Liff for her keen ability to translate my artistic vision into the actual layout of the book. Last, but surely not least, thanks to Rabbi Moshe Dombey for his ongoing encouragement and overall support.

Special thanks to Rabbi Zev Leff for his beautifully written *haskamah* for the book. I hope I will be able to live up to his many blessings.

The unsung hero of this book is Menachem Butler, who, after hearing the kernel ideas of the book at a lecture in New York City, exclaimed, "You must write this lecture up." He was so sincere and enthusiastic that I more or less decided on the spot that this would be my next major project.

The essential ideas in this book were transmitted over a few years in various lectures, *Shabbatonim*, musical get-togethers, and around my Shabbat table to students and audiences in the context of my ongoing work with Ohr Chadash: New Horizons in Jewish Experience (see the last page in this book for a detailed description of our educational work). The best way to learn is to teach, and I am very grateful to have the privilege of being in contact with so many wonderful people in cities all over North America and throughout Israel.

My deep appreciation to those whose dedications to loved ones helped in making this project possible. To Ken and Vicki Pepper and their wonderful children, who have been so close to me; to Rabbi Henoch Dov and Sari Hoffman and family, who have been dear and supportive friends for so long; and to Brahm and Lynn Silverstone and their children Rabbi Chaim and Chaya Silverstone, with whom I have shared so much these past few years. To all of you, thank you for your support and vote of confidence.

Since this book is so connected to my work with Ohr Chadash, I would like to thank all those who have contributed in so many ways, including some very special people whose recent generous support and assistance have allowed Ohr Chadash to grow and thrive: Michael and Barbara Katch, Ze'ev and Chaya London, Steven Alevy, Chuck and Betty Whiting, Zvi and Sharon Gelt, Fred and Karen Pasternack, Scott and Sally Alpert, and Elana Friedman. May you get lots of *nachas* from our ongoing educational work.

Special thanks and praise go to Marty and Chavi Lee, whose unshakable commitment to the vision and programs of Ohr Chadash has been instrumental in our development. Even more is the true warmth and caring that goes along with everything they do. To say we couldn't do it without them would be an understatement.

I would like to express my deep appreciation to Rabbi Shlomo Carlebach, who opened the gates of Jewish music for me and whose songs have penetrated virtually the entire Jewish world and beyond. This book is in great part a written expression of the vital effect of these melodies on my heart and soul.

I am most humbly grateful to Rabbi Yitzchak Ginsburgh for permission to include his many teachings quoted throughout this book. These teachings inspired me greatly and created the incentive to delve deeply into the mystical power of music. The unified vision of reality expressed in many ways throughout the book is a product of thirty years of study with Rabbi Ginsburgh, and for this I am eternally grateful.

To my wife Rachel, who shares with me day in and day out our life's work and dreams, and to my children Dvaria, Efrayim Dovid, and Chana Shira, the joys of my life: to them all I owe my sense of being who I am. They give me the strength to always go forward with joy in my life and a melody in my heart.

And to the Ribbono shel Olam, the Master of the World, to whom all praise is due and from whom all music ultimately emanates. For God is the Composer, the Singer, and the Song. Please open my lips (and heart, mind, and soul) that my mouth should forever sing Your praises.

Introduction

usic, perhaps more than any other medium, has the unique ability to express and mirror the full range of human emotions, consciousness, and experience. Its appeal on one hand is universal, transcending race, religion, culture, and era, while on the other hand nothing captures the particular essence of a specific culture, religion, era, or individual better than music. It allows the soul to soar to heavenly heights, giving wing to man's most glorious aspirations and dreams. It expresses as well man's greatest pain, sadness, and existential loneliness.

Who has not experienced themselves singing full volume in the shower or along with every word of a song on the car radio or at home while all alone? Who has not been depressed or lonely, joyous or happy to be alive and found in a tape or CD the very songs to express these moods? Who has not sat around with friends and experienced through song and melodic harmony a unity of soul and purpose as voices and instruments joined together? Who has not felt the raw power and mystic connection at a concert where everyone is locked into the same beat, the same vibrational field? Or the connection at a large public event where hundreds or thousands of people are all connected and focused through the same song? And who has not felt in the special melodies used during the various Jewish holidays the essence and intrinsic meaning these days are meant to impart to us?

Music without words plays on the chords of the heart and the fantasy of the mind. Music with words expresses the deepest longings, challenges, and hopes of a human being. Not only does it move the soul to joyous laughter or deeply felt tears, but the body as well is caught up in its driving beat. Music is a cosmic language that unites the physical and spiritual, body and soul, universal and particular, while simultaneously transcending time and temporal space altogether.

This book hopes to delve into the different qualities of music and the deeper reasons of why it exerts such a strong influence on both body and soul, effecting us in such profound ways. To accomplish this we will bring a wide array of sources from Jewish tradition; from the Tanach (the five books of Moses, the prophets and the writings) to the full spectrum of oral Torah, including Kabbalistic and Chassidic teachings. In addition, we will draw upon sources from the natural world and science in an attempt to bring an understanding and unified vision to the underlying meaning of music. In the process we will probe the very essence of creation and the nature of physical and spiritual reality itself.

We are taught that there are seventy facets to the Torah (*BeMidbar Rabbah* 13:15), each one representing a legitimate perspective of the Torah and the world we live in. The Arizal, the great sixteenth century Kabbalist from Safed, mentions 600,000 facets, one for each archetypal Jewish root soul. The following teachings, drawn from many different sources, coalesced in my thoughts over

Introduction • 17

a long period of time and represent just one way to look at the mystical power of music. I hope it will resonate with you, the reader, as it does for me. Even more so, I pray it will spark your own stream of consciousness, connecting ideas I have not mentioned or even thought of. For this is the way of Torah and this is the vibrancy and symphony of our oral tradition.

Music in the Jewish Tradition

ing David, the archetypal king of Israel, is called "the sweet singer of Israel" (Samuel II 23:1). In addition to being a leader of the people, a warrior, and a devoted student of Torah, he was also a poet and musician. One can imagine how this quality was enhanced by his years of herding sheep in virtual solitude in the deserts and pastures of the land of Israel. He had long stretches of time to hear the song of nature and to commune with God. These experiences no doubt contributed greatly to the psalms of David, which are by far the most widely known and most influential songs in history. I say "songs" purposely because, though many people are used to reading or reciting the psalms as verse or poetry, they were originally written by David as songs.

A fundamental part of prayer and ritual, the psalms' influence pervaded Jewish thought and culture throughout the generations.

The unique relationship between David and God, as described and recorded through the medium of music and poetry, has had a lasting effect on our relationship to God. Christianity and its various churches have incorporated the psalms into their services and ritual, and secular Western culture, literature, and music is full of examples of the lasting influence of the psalms. David is considered a prophet in Islam as well.

David's musical abilities are described in the book of Samuel. When King Saul did not kill Aggag, the king of Amalek, after a critical battle, against an explicit command of God, God sent Samuel to inform Saul that the kingship would be taken away from him. At the command of God, Samuel then anointed David in secret to be the new king, and "the spirit of God came upon David from that day onwards" (Samuel I 16:13). The *Meam Loez* on this verse brings the tradition that "from that day on" all the songs and lyrics of David were written in a spirit of Divine inspiration and prophecy.

When King Saul's servants saw that an "evil spirit" had come upon him, they advised him to find someone who knew how to play music in order to calm his troubled soul. Saul agreed and asked them to find someone who could not only play an instrument but also could sing lyrics that would bring him peace (*Meam Loez* on Samuel I 16:17). It was then reported to him that David was such a person and he was brought to the king for that purpose. When an evil spirit would come upon Saul, he would call for David to play for him, and the music would calm and heal his tormented soul.

We see from this story that music was considered a type of healing and therapy, something virtually every person can relate to. Many times listening to certain music when depressed or troubled has an immediate and soothing effect on the soul. And as Saul knew also, the words that go with the music are sometimes what reach us so deeply. Yet if we read those very words without music it is doubtful that they would have nearly the same effect.

The Connection between Music and Divine Inspiration

Although there are many ways that Divine spirit and prophecy manifest themselves, it is significant that music is one of those ways. We see this clearly in another story involving Saul, who was also anointed by Samuel. At first, Saul was quite taken aback at being chosen as the first king of Israel, but Samuel assured him that it was ordained on High and gave him a number of signs of things that would happen to him to prove that indeed he was meant to be king. Among those signs, he was told that "you will meet a band of prophets coming down from the high place with a lute and a timbrel, and a pipe and a lyre before them, and they shall prophesy and the spirit of God will come upon you and you will prophesy with them and you shall be turned into another man" (Samuel I 9:5–11).

Saul in fact does meet the band of prophets and he too begins to prophesy. It is explained that the band of prophets used music as the means to create the proper spiritual atmosphere in which the Divine spirit could come upon them.

Later in history Elisha, one of the greatest miracle workers in the Bible, was asked by three kings to inquire of God what to do.

He requested that they bring him a minstrel, and the prophet records, "And it came to pass when the minstrel played, the hand of God came upon him" (Kings II 3:15). It is further recorded in the book of Chronicles I (25:1) that Asaph, Heman, and Jeduthun "would prophesy with the harp, lute, and cymbal."

It is clear that Jewish mystics in all ages knew the unique ability of music to create spiritual experiences and enable a person to enter a deep meditative state of consciousness. A state of prophecy only comes through joy, and that is the essential connection between prophecy and music; for nothing awakens, fuels, and expresses joy more than music.

For this reason we are taught that Jacob lost the spirit of prophecy during the twenty-two years that he thought his son Joseph was dead. His state of mourning prevented any real joy to enter his soul, thereby cutting off the possibility of Divine inspiration.

The Torah states that, immediately upon hearing that Joseph was in fact alive, "the spirit of Jacob...was revived" (Genesis 48:27). The *Targum Onkelos*, the Aramaic translation, writes that at that moment the spirit of prophecy was revived in Jacob. As soon as his mourning stopped and joy returned to his heart, so too did the spirit of prophecy.

Music Rooted in the Higher Spheres

We are taught that David never slept a whole night through; rather he would take short naps to refresh himself. Each night he would sleep till midnight, when a north wind would blow through his harp hanging above his bed. The wind blowing on the strings would play a melody which awakened him. The rest of the night he spent learning, playing music, and communing with God. We can imagine that it was on one of these nights that David composed the words: "I will sing and give praise. Wake up, my glory, awake the harp and the lyre; I will awaken the dawn" (Psalms 57:9).

It is significant that it was specifically a north wind that played on David's harp because the word "north," *tzafon*, also means "hidden." This alludes to the idea that music and song ultimately come from a lofty, hidden, spiritual realm. Music, in turn, awakens in a person his or her more hidden, subconscious level of soul, which is ultimately rooted in God.

In Kabbalah, music is associated with *keter*, the "crown," the highest and most hidden of the ten *sefirot*, the Divine emanations, through which an infinite God creates and maintains a finite world. Just as the full DNA code appears in virtually every cell of the body, so too, according to Kabbalah, do the ten *sefirot* manifest themselves in every point of time and space. (The ten *sefirot*, the model and paradigm of all existence, will be mentioned periodically throughout the book as a way to understand the nature of music and ultimately reality itself.)

Keter, the highest of the *sefirot*, relates to the subconscious and superconscious levels of the soul. Just as a crown sits upon a head, so do the more subconscious and superconscious aspects of the soul "sit" upon the head, the more conscious intellect. There are in fact three aspects of *keter*: faith, spiritual pleasure, and will. Music relates to all of these aspects, as shall be explained later on in this book.

Music in the Temple

Although David did not actually build the Temple, it was he who first thought of building a House for God. When David tells the prophet Gad of his desire to build such a place to house the ark of God, God reveals to Gad that although David will not merit to build it, his son will. More than this, though, because of David's concern for His glory, God promises to establish David's kingdom forever. This is one of the scriptural sources for the teaching that the Messiah, who will serve as king of Israel, will come from the house of David.

The book of Samuel describes how David brought the ark of God up to Jerusalem for the first time, thus paving the way for the building of the Temple: "So David went and brought up the ark of God from the house of Obed-edom into the city of David with gladness.... And David leaped about before God with all his might and David was girded with a linen ephod. So David and all the House of Israel brought up the ark of God with shouting and with the sound of the shofar" (Samuel II 6:12–15).

David wrote in prophecy: "A psalm; a song of the dedication of the Temple by David" (Psalms 30:1). This psalm is recited every day in our prayers and is included in the ritual for dedicating a new house until this very day. The fact that David dedicated the Temple with a song is very significant, since the Temple experience was the central paradigm of Jewish service of God.

Although the Temple was destroyed nearly two thousand years ago, the Sages were able to take all the main components of the physical Temple and the service that was performed there throughout the year and translate them into our various prayer services and the physical makeup of our synagogues today. It is beyond the scope of this book to delve extensively into this subject, but the order, timing, and content of the daily, Shabbat, and holiday services include many aspects of the Temple service as it was performed two thousand years ago. Even the physical structure of the synagogue and its main symbols and motifs mirror the structure of the Temple.

For example, the *bimah*, the central table in the synagogue, represents the outer altar where the sacrifices were offered. We are taught that our prayers today are a direct replacement of those offerings. The *aron kodesh*, the ark, containing the Torah scrolls, represents the Torah scroll and the tablets of the law that rested in the ark in the Holy of Holies, and the curtain in front of the *aron kodesh* today represents the curtain in front of the Holy of Holies. The *ner tamid*, the everlasting light, in the synagogue represents the seven-branched menorah, the candelabrum. Our synagogues all face Jerusalem in memory of the Temple itself. The *mechitzah*, or divider, of today is modeled on the separation made by the Sages in certain areas of the Temple in order to separate men and women.

As for the prayers, the morning and afternoon services we pray replace the *tamid*, the morning and afternoon daily offerings. The evening prayer replaces the offerings that burned on the altar all night. The *mussaf*, or additional prayer on Shabbat and holidays, replaces the additional offerings brought on these days. Each morning we recite *korbanot*, the readings about the Temple offerings, at the very beginning of prayer, to emphasize the essential connection between the offerings and our prayers today. *Pesukei DeZimrah*, the verses of song, correspond to the songs of the Levites in the Temple. In Israel, the priests bless the congregation every day, as they did daily in the Temple. (Outside of Israel the priestly blessing is recited daily by the prayer leader, and the priests bless the congregation only on holidays.) Each day we read the particular song the Levites sang in the Temple. *Tachanun*, verses of repentance, replace the guilt offering, while *Mizmor LeTodah*, a song of thanksgiving, symbolizes the thanksgiving offering. These are just some of the many examples.

Not only do our services and prayers reflect the Temple model, but the Jewish collective consciousness also remembers and longs for the Temple, which is not just a potent symbol of national and religious sovereignty but actually the place where we experienced the Divine Presence. The experience of being in the Temple was so powerful that even a two-thousand-year absence cannot wipe out that collective memory.

The wondrous music that was played in the Temple constantly was central to the spiritual experience. King David wrote fifteen Songs of Ascent, corresponding to the fifteen future steps in the Temple, where the greatest choir and orchestra ever assembled in the history of the world sang and played. The men of the tribe of Levi trained vigorously till age thirty before taking their place among the multitude of musicians who performed there. People came to the Temple with great expectations and high emotions, completely focused on drawing close to God, and the music which took place there was an integral part of the spiritual experience.

The Mishnah recounts the joyous music and singing during *simchat beit haSho'eivah*, the drawing of the water ceremony, which took place in the Temple every Sukkot, the seven-day harvest pilgrimage festival. The Sages describe how water was festively drawn each day from a spring in Jerusalem, brought in a great procession to the altar, and poured out to symbolize our prayer for rain and sustenance. The entire evening the great Sages of the generation would lead joyous singing, dancing, and praising of God to the accompaniment of the Levites, who, according to the Mishnah, played on instruments too numerous to count. The joy at these celebrations was so great that the Mishnah states: "Anyone who has not seen *simchat beit hasho'eivah* has never really seen true joy" (Mishnah, *Sukkah* 5:1).

The very next *mishnah* recalls how each day of the year there were never less than twenty-one series of shofar blasts in the Temple and never more than forty-eight. The shofar which we know so well from Rosh HaShanah was played by experts like a musical instrument. The Levites would also accompany all the daily offerings on the altar with song. Every holiday, Hallel, a special arrangement of joyous praises of God, was sung in the Temple and the Levites would play and sing.

Another *mishnah* recalls how the Levites sang a special song appropriate for each day of the week, a practice incorporated into our prayers today (*Tamid* 7:3). It is stated that the sound of the shofar and the Levites playing and singing could be heard as far away as Jericho, many miles away (Mishnah, *Tamid* 3:8).

Part of the clothing of the high priest was a robe which had bells sewn along the bottom seam. As he performed his daily service they made a faint, tinkling, musical sound.

The bringing of the first fruits was a major celebration in Jerusalem. Very large processions of people would ascend with great rejoicing to Jerusalem, walking to the sound of flutes, with their first fruits in decorated baskets. The people of Jerusalem would come to greet them and accompany the procession to the Temple, where the Levites would break forth in joyous song (Mishnah, B*ikurim* 3:2–4).

When the Levites played and sang at each of the above events, the visitors to the Temple experienced peak moments of awe and spiritual elevation. These experiences left a deep mark on all those individuals who attended and upon the collective consciousness of the Jewish people. As Saul, through the medium of the music of the band of prophets, "became another man," so, too, all those who came to the Temple were spiritually elevated. Music not just enhanced the daily service, but was an integral and fundamental component of it, and this fact has had a major effect on the prayers we say today, as will be explained in the next chapter.

Today, many have life-changing experiences when visiting the Kotel, the Western Wall, which is but an outside retaining wall below where the Temple was located. How much greater must have been the experience in the Temple itself! It is no wonder that prayers for rebuilding Jerusalem and the Temple are included in so many contemporary prayers and rituals, as we long for a return of this reality to our lives.

The Ten Archetypal Songs

David's time period is not the first mention of music and song in the Bible. Even in the very beginning of the book of Genesis, where the first generations of man are recounted, musical instruments are mentioned: "And Lemech took two wives; the name of one was Ada and the name of the other Zilla. And Ada gave birth to Jabal, he was the father of those who dwell in tents and of such that have cattle. And his brother was Jubal; he was the father of all who handle the lyre and the pipe. And Zilla also gave birth to Tubal-Cain, forger of every sharp instrument in brass and iron…" (Genesis 4:19–22). The fact that musical instruments are one of the only human achievements mentioned in the first seven generations of man emphasizes music's obvious importance.

According to tradition there are ten archetypal songs sung throughout history. These songs stand out among all the other countless songs in Jewish tradition in that each one was written in a state of Divine inspiration or prophecy and came at a climactic moment of transition, transformation, or revelation for an individual or all the people. They all reflect to some degree a high level of awareness of God's Providence, a sense of mission and purpose, and a feeling of completion and wholeness. They are the expression of those rare and unique moments in life when everything seems to fall into place, when everything feels perfect, just as it should be. During such moments, everything about life makes sense and we feel an immediate urge to thank and praise God.

As we will see, these songs accompany history from Adam, the first human, to the Messiah, who will lead Israel and all the world to the consummate and final redemption. These songs, enumerated by the *Targum Yonatan* in his commentary on the first verse of the Song of Songs, were sung by both men and women, kings and judges, individuals and the entire people.

The first song was sung by Adam after his expulsion from the Garden of Eden. According to the Midrash (*Bereishit Rabbah* 22:28), Adam came to Cain after he killed Abel and asked how God had judged him. Cain said that he repented and God made a "compromise" with him. After God decreed upon Cain that he would be a fugitive and wander the earth, Cain cried out that his punishment was greater than he could bear, and at that point he repented for what he had done. "God then said: 'Therefore, whoever slays Cain vengeance will be taken on him sevenfold.' And God set a mark upon Cain in order that none who found him should smite him" (Genesis 4:10–15).

The Slonimer Rebbe (*Netivot Shalom*, Genesis, p. 29) quotes an explanation of the "compromise" between God and Cain by the Rebbe of Milkovitz, who explains that the word for the "mark" God set upon Cain is in Hebrew the same word as "sign." Shabbat is also called a "sign," as in the verse: "Therefore the children of Israel shall keep the Shabbat, to observe the Shabbat throughout their generations, for a perpetual covenant. It is a sign between Me and the children of Israel forever" (Exodus 31:16–17). The "compromise," according to the Rebbe of Milkovitz, was that since his killing Abel could not be totally wiped away, during the week his punishment was to wander as a fugitive, but in reward for repenting he would find rest and peace of mind on Shabbat.

The above *midrash* continues by saying that Adam, when he heard this, hit himself on the head and said: "This is the power of repentance and I didn't know it!" Immediately he stood up and exclaimed: "A psalm, a song for the day of Shabbat. It is good to thank God and to sing praise to Your name" (Psalms 92:1). This psalm of individual revelation has been incorporated into our evening and morning Shabbat prayers.

The second song was sung by Moses and all of Israel after crossing the Reed Sea and seeing the Egyptians drown in the sea. This marks the final act of leaving Egypt and the culmination of generations of slavery and oppression (Exodus 15:1–19). We are taught that the revelation of God at the sea was so great that what the simplest handmaiden witnessed was greater than even the revelations of Ezekiel the prophet (*Shir HaShirim Rabbah* 3:9). The revelation all the people experienced was transformed into spontaneous joy and song. The Torah describes how Moses led the men in song and the women added music and dancing, as the Torah states: "And Miriam the prophetess, the sister of Aaron, took a timbrel in her hand and all the women went out after her with timbrels and dances" (Exodus 15:20–21). The song of the sea is included in our daily prayers every morning (*Az Yashir*).

The third song was song by all of Israel upon receiving water in the desert: "Then Israel sang this song: 'Spring up O well; sing to it; the well the princes dug out, that the nobles of the people delved, with the scepter, with their staves' " (Numbers 21:17). Water is life, especially in the desert. In addition, we are taught that whenever water is mentioned in the Bible it is an allusion to Torah, which is also called a "Torah of life" (Proverbs 4:2). There are numerous mentions of water in the narratives of the patriarchs and matriarchs and the narratives of the life of Moses and the forty years in the desert. Here, the joy of receiving water on all its various levels of meaning, produced a song by all the nation.

The fourth song, H*a*A*zinu*, was sung by Moses at the end of his life as a culminating review of the history of the world and the Jewish people, replete with predictions and prophecies for the future (Deuteronomy 32:1–43). According to Ramban and many other commentators, this song contains the secrets of each individual and generation from the days of Moses until the time of the Messiah.

The fifth song was sung by Joshua after the miraculous and climactic event of the stopping of the sun and the moon: "Then Joshua spoke to God on the day when God had delivered up the Emori before the children of Israel; and he said in the sight of Israel: 'Sun, stand still in Gibeon, and moon, [stand still] in the Valley of Aijalon.' And the sun stood still and the moon stayed until the people had avenged themselves upon their enemies.... So the sun stood still in the middle of the sky and hastened not to go down about a whole day. And there was no day before this or after it that God hearkened to the voice of a man..." (Joshua 10:12–14). Joshua, according to tradition, was able to stop the sun and moon by actually singing their song.

The sixth song was sung by Deborah and Barak after God delivered Sisera into their hands and they inflicted a decisive victory over Jabin, the king of Canaan. Deborah was both a prophetess and judge in Israel, who "dwelt under the palm tree of Deborah between Rama and Beth-El in Mount Ephraim, and the children of Israel came to her for judgment" (Judges 4:5). Her song (recorded in Judges, ch. 5) concludes with the statement that the victory over Sisera was so great that it was followed by forty years of peace in the land.

The seventh song was sung by Hannah, mother of the

prophet Samuel, who was unable to bear a child for many years and suffered terribly because of her barrenness. After a heartfelt prayer to God to give her a son, whom she promised she would dedicate to God, she became pregnant with Samuel. The Sages learn a number of important principles from Hannah's prayer, which are incorporated into the laws of prayer to this day. After she gave birth, she sang a song of thanksgiving (Samuel I 2:1–10).

The eighth song was sung by David as a culminating expression of thanks: "And David spoke to God the words of this song on the day that God delivered him out of the hand of all his enemies, and out of the hand of Saul" (Samuel II 22:1–51). Part of the closing line of the song has been incorporated into the Grace after Meals: "He is the tower of salvation for His king and shows mercy to His anointed, David, and to his seed forever." Although David wrote many songs which are recorded in the book of Psalms, only this one has the status of one of the ten songs of history. It is written in the Torah in the unique form of a song, similar to the way the song of the sea and HaAzinu are written in a Torah scroll.

The ninth song, the Song of Songs, was written by King Solomon, who according to the *Zohar* was inspired to compose it on the day he inaugurated the first Temple in Jerusalem. Due to its great depths of meaning and the fact that its allegorical nature is couched in the guise of a passionate love story, the Sages considered leaving it out of the Bible when it was canonized. Rabbi Akiva, the greatest sage of his generation, disagreed and stated that all the books of Scripture are holy, but the Song of Songs is the holy of holies (*Midrash Tanchuma, Tetzaveh* 8). This great love story can be understood on many different levels, especially as the consummate description of the love between God and the Jewish people. Its verses have profoundly influenced Jewish art, music, poetry, and literature, and by extension the Western and Islamic world as well. In this sense it can truly be called the "Song of Songs."

The tenth song is awaiting the Messiah and the final redemption, when the exiles returning home will "sing a new song to God." This final song represents a time when the purpose of human history will be revealed and all peoples of the earth will worship God as one. This joyous song will express a totally new understanding of life and represents the ultimate sense of completion, purpose, and wholeness, the very definition of song.

We see from these songs that music accompanies mankind from its inception till the awaited Messianic era. As pure expressions of the soul, these songs have been faithfully recorded and made an integral part of Jewish tradition and ritual.

Throughout the generations, and especially during the nearly two millennium of exile, song has accompanied the Jewish people. The great poets of the golden ages of Babylon and Spain (from the beginning of the common era to the fifteenth century) bequeathed to us *piyutim*, special poetic songs integrated into our holiday prayers, as well as *kinnot*, lamentations recited on Tishah B'Av, the day set aside for mourning the destruction of the Temple and our state of exile. In the past thousand years, various sages have composed *zemirot*, the special songs of Shabbat which we sing at each of the three meals on that day. These songs, compiled over many generations and in many different locales, symbolize the Jewish people's ongoing development and expression of self in music and song.

Our great leaders, judges, kings, prophets, sages, rabbis, and mystics have used, and still use, music in various ways to express the deepest longings of the heart, to heal the spirit, to receive Divine inspiration, and to praise God. Music is the quill of the soul, expressing the most Divine aspect of the individual, the Jewish people, and humanity. It records the past, captures the present, and envisions the future, sometimes all at once. In this sense, music allows us to experience the very essence of eternity.

Music, Song, and Prayer

n the Hebrew language each letter is associated with a number, and in Kabbalah it is taught that the numerical sum of all the letters of a word has great meaning. When two words share the same numerical value it is understood that they are connected in some essential manner. The word for "song" in Hebrew is *shirah*, equaling 515, the same number as the word for prayer, *tefillah*. This is not a mere casual connection, but rather a fundamental lesson on the essence of prayer and song. Another beautiful numerical connection between prayer and song is that there are ten synonyms for prayer (*Devarim Rabbah* 2:1) and there are ten synonyms for song in the book of Psalms (*Pesachim* 117a).

The essential relationship between prayer and song is expressed in numerous ways in the prayers themselves. The preliminary blessings and readings of the morning service are followed by the section called *Pesukei DeZimrah*, verses of song, comprised of, for the most part, the psalms of David. These psalms and other additions are full of praise for the Creator and mention over and over the need to praise God with song:

> A psalm of thanksgiving, call out to God, everyone on earth. Serve God with gladness, come before Him with joyous song.
>
> (Psalms 100:1–2)
>
> Halleluyah! Praise God, O my soul! I will praise God while I live, I will make music to my God while I exist.
>
> (Psalms 146:1–2)
>
> Halleluyah! For it is good to make music to our God, for praise is pleasant and befitting.
>
> (Psalms 147:1)
>
> Halleluyah! Sing to God a new song, let His praise be in the congregation of the devout. Let Israel exalt in its Maker, let the children of Israel rejoice in its King.
>
> (Psalms 149:1–2)
>
> Praise Him with the blast of the shofar; praise Him with lyre and harp. Praise Him with drum and dance; praise Him with organ and flute. Praise Him with clanging cymbals; praise Him with resonant trumpets....
>
> (Psalms 150:3–5)

Near the end of *Pesukei DeZimrah* is one of the ten archetypal songs, the song of the sea, reminding us in a symbolic manner that the challenges and obstacles of each day are like a sea we need to cross. What a wonderful attitude — to face those challenges with song in our heart!

The closing blessing of this segment of the service is an elegant summation of all the above sentiments:

> Blessed are You, God, a King exalted and lauded through praises, God of thanksgiving, Master of wonders, creator of all souls, Master of all deeds, who chooses musical songs of praise; King, Unique One, God, Life-Giver of the world.

The next section of prayer contains the blessings before and after the Shema, the cardinal statement of faith in one God. Here too there are many references to song, but this time it is the angels and heavenly beings who are praising God:

> And they all open their mouth in holiness and purity, in song and hymn, and bless, praise, glorify, revere, sanctify and declare the kingship of the name of God....

> To the blessed God they shall offer sweet melodies; to the King, the living and enduring God, they shall sing hymns and utter praises.

The above are just a few of the many examples of the references to music, song, and the joy in serving God in our daily prayers. The Shabbat and holiday prayers are likewise filled with joyous references to song, musical instruments and praise of God.

Serving God through Prayer and Song

When King David, the "sweet singer of Israel," exclaimed: "And I am prayer" (Psalms 109:4), he was saying, in essence, "Prayer is not something I do — it is what I am." David was in a constant dialogue with God, whether he was on the top of the world or in the lowest hell — he was always praising, singing, talking to, pleading with, crying to, and reaching out to God. David combined music, song, praise, confession, and prayer, blurring the lines between them. Just as David's all-encompassing consciousness was prayer, so was it music and song. For David brought music and prayer together as one.

The Temple experience, as mentioned above, continued the tradition of using music, song, and dance in the service of God. The two Temples stood for over eight hundred years of our history and their impression is deeply ingrained in Jewish thought and practice throughout the ages.

Unfortunately, though, the long and crushing exile took its toll, affecting the nation's ability to carry on the joyous service of God. Though we miraculously were able to survive as a people and carry on faithfully the Torah tradition, it seems the essential connection between prayer and music weakened along the way. For the most part the prayers and psalms became something to recite, not sing, and usually as quickly as possible. Prayer became for more and more people an obligation, not a spiritual opportunity and fulfilling experience.

In the 1700s a charismatic teacher, the Baal Shem Tov, railed against the rote performance of mitzvot, commandments, in general and especially against the nearly total lack of joy in the communal prayers of many of the common folk of his day. He reinforced the idea of serving God with joy and the essential importance of music and singing in awakening the heart and soul. He put great emphasis on making both individual and communal prayer an uplifting, moving experience, igniting a virtual spiritual revolution.

Yet, like all revolutions, the initial flames of excitement stoked by the Baal Shem Tov also diminished in intensity. In the last few generations, the lack of spiritual depth, enthusiasm, and joy in the typical synagogue experience has contributed greatly to the decreased interest in Jewish traditions and roots, fueling an estrangement and assimilation of catastrophic proportions.

One of the most notable people who stepped into this situation was Rabbi Shlomo Carlebach, *z"l*, who devoted much of his life to trying to awaken the slumbering spark of innate holiness in the Jewish heart through music, joy, and a more meaningful and spiritual prayer experience. For nearly forty years he traveled the world, using his songs, teachings, and particular way of leading the prayers to inspire others with a renewed sense of how meaningful and uplifting the synagogue experience could be. The fact that so many congregations have incorporated his songs and spirit into their services tells us what a great vacuum needed filling.

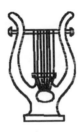

Music and Prayer as Connection

Throughout Jewish history, music and song have been employed as an instrument to bring people together in an effective and powerful expression of community. The prayer services in our synagogues are meant to capture the sense of awe and community which existed in the Holy Temple. Especially in a fast-lane, technological, 24/7 world, where people feel more and more isolated and lacking in direction and purpose, a feeling of Jewish community and sharing takes on a new immediacy and importance. So many people, especially the young, who want to connect to their Jewish roots but cannot find a sense of community or spiritual connection to Judaism, are being attracted to the invigorating freshness and depths of music and prayer connecting in a communal setting.

Another way that music has been used throughout the ages is as an aid to meditation. Jewish meditation is practiced in many forms, including the enhancement of prayer and study. Meditation has many of the elements of prayer and music, and at times the three unite in perfect harmony. This idea was also emphasized greatly by the Baal Shem Tov and is an important component to the teachings of the Chassidic movement.

A *niggun* (wordless song), a prayer, or a verse of Torah sung over and over again can focus the mind and bring the ego to a state of self-nullification. Music can take us soaring to unimaginable heights of inner peace and ecstasy. Alternatively, music can be used as a catalyst to focus one's mind on particular intentions, emotions, or concepts, allowing new insight and revelation to manifest themselves. Ultimately, music is a potent vehicle to feeling at one and at peace with God. The act of unifying with God is the deepest drive of the Jewish soul, and prayer and song have been used throughout Jewish tradition and ritual as a means to achieve this lofty state of consciousness.

The period prior to the Messianic era is referred to as the "footsteps of the Messiah," implying that as the era draws near we will experience events that are like the sound of faint footsteps in the distance, growing louder and louder as they get closer and closer. The renewal of song and joyous prayer in our day, as more and more Jews are moving to Israel, reminds us of the tenth archetypal song the exiles will sing as they return to their ancient homeland. We cannot yet hear the full song, but the faint outline of the tune is getting perceptively louder. May we merit to hear and sing it quickly in our days!

Torah and the Song of the Creator

ach and every morning we recite the following words as part of the morning service: "Blessed is the One who spoke and the world came into being." Are these words meant to be taken literally or figuratively? Is it an allegorical image or is there a reality behind the words?

In *Pirkei Avot*, The Ethics of the Fathers, it is written: "With ten utterances the world was created" (*Avot* 5:1). *Pirkei Avot*, far from being considered a mystical treatise, is a collection of ethical and moral teachings from the Sages. The normative tradition as brought in *Pirkei Avot* is that the instrument through which God created the world was Divine speech.

When one reads the Torah account of creation, it is clear where this tradition comes from. On the first day of creation it is written, "And God said, 'Let there be light' — and there was light" (Genesis 1:3). The pattern of a Divine utterance, followed immediately by the creation of the very thing spoken about in the utterance, is repeated throughout creation. The oral Torah, handed down along with the written Torah, takes the idea of Divine speech as the instrument of creation quite literally.

Further, we are taught that creation is actually constructed from the Hebrew letters, considered the building blocks of creation. Similar to a scientist who would describe the building blocks of creation as atoms, molecules, and elements, our tradition views the Hebrew letters as the very foundation of the universe. The letters that form the word for any particular entity or action in the Torah are more than linguistic symbols — they are the animating Divine force forming its actual essence and basic reality. Therefore, the letters that make up the word for "light," for example, are what light actually is. Not only are the letters the building blocks of creation, but the Torah is considered the actual blueprint of creation, as is taught in the *Zohar* (2:161b): "God looked into the Torah and created the world."

Just as today we know of the incredible energy packed into an infinitesimally small atom, the Hebrew letters are intensely contracted conduits of Divine light and energy, serving as the channels of Divine speech. In the Divine creative process speech is action — there is no separation between the two.

In human terms we can understand this to a certain degree when considering the various results of our own speech. We know how words spoken in anger or on impulse can instantaneously pierce through the heart, destroy a life-long relationship in a minute, ruin a reputation, cause murder, or lead nations to war. In the more positive sense, compassionate and loving speech can heal wounds, give strength to the weary, resurrect hope, and inspire masses of people.

The ten utterances of creation are essentially connected to

the ten archetypal songs sung throughout history. They are the more human face of the same basic cosmological energy. Each of these structures of ten encompasses the full array of its respective realms of creation and human history. In turn, both sets of ten are clearly interconnected with the ten *sefirot*, the basic model of all existence, from the physical to the spiritual.

One other model of ten that needs mentioning is the Ten Commandments, the quintessential "kernel" of all the commandments in the Torah. The idea of the Ten Commandments representing all the commandments can be seen in a beautiful mathematical gem. There are 613 commandments in the Torah, as well as seven universal commandments known as the seven commandments of the children of Noah. Together they equal 620, the exact number of letters in the Ten Commandments!

The word *keter*, crown, also equals 620. In many synagogues around the world the curtain hanging before the ark where the Torah is kept is decorated with a crown, as are many mantels adorning the Torah scroll itself. Additionally, many congregations put a silver crown on the Torah when it is taken out of the ark. *Keter* in Kabbalah represents the subconscious and superconscious source of intellect. This is considered the source of music and song in the soul, as discussed above.

Significantly, the Torah itself is called song. After God revealed through Moses the blessing and the curse and the prophecies concerning the future of the Jewish people, God taught him the song *HaAzinu*, whose teachings were to be impressed upon all the people: "And now write this song for yourselves and teach it to the children of Israel..." (Deuteronomy 31:19). The oral Torah explains that this verse refers not only to the song of *HaAzinu*, but also to the obligation of each individual to write the entire Torah. From this we learn that all the Torah is considered song!

In the context of a discussion in the Talmud concerning the importance of learning Torah and reviewing it, Rabbi Akiva is quoted as saying, "Sing every day, sing every day" (*Sanhedrin* 99a–b). Rashi explains that even if one has reviewed his learning he should sing it in order that it accompany him to the next world in joy and song.

Singing the Torah means to fully integrate its teachings and wisdom into our hearts and our minds. We must connect the Torah we learn to our most essential being and not treat it as an intellectual pastime or pursuit. Singing our Torah connects its teachings to our deepest selves.

The Inner Dynamics of Creation

One of the methods used by Kabbalah to delve into deeper and deeper levels of Torah understanding is permuting letters of words to find associated connections and correspondences. Through this exercise we become aware of the inner dynamics and essence of the word. A classic work of Kabbalah, the *Tikunei Zohar*, uses this method, taking the first word of the Torah, *bereishit*, "in the beginning," and permuting its six letters to reveal profound secrets of the very mechanics of creation.

One of the combinations of the letters of *bereishit* is שירת אב, "the song of the father" or "the cardinal/essential song." The letters of אב, "father," are the two initial letters of the *alef-beit*, the Hebrew alphabet. Thus, another way of reading the above combination of letters would be "the song of the *alef-beit*." These two combinations of letters of the opening word of the Torah reveal an awesome insight — the Divine speech of our Father in Heaven was in fact song, the song of the *alef-beit*, the Hebrew letters. God in effect sang the world into existence!!

Another permutation of the letters of *bereishit* is שיר תאב, "the passionate song." This permutation relates to the enigmatic statement explaining the purpose of creation: "God desired to have for Himself a dwelling place in the lower worlds" (*Midrash Tanchuma*,

Naso 16). The world, the product of Divine song, is mysteriously the object of God's desire for a dwelling place below.

The commandment to write a Torah scroll is considered the last of the 613 commandments. The Torah and creation begin with "the song of the father," "the song of the *alef-beit*," "the cardinal/essential song," while the last and concluding commandment is to write the entire Torah, which is called "song." This fulfills what is written in the *Sefer Yetzirah* (1:7), the first classic book of Kabbalah: "Their end is embedded in their beginning and their beginning in the end."

We are taught that there are four basic levels to learning Torah text. The acronym for these four levels is פרדס, which means "orchard." Beginning from the lowest of these levels, the פ is for *peshat*, the literal meaning; the ר is for *remez*, the hinted or alluded to meaning; the ד is for *drush*, the homiletic or allegorical meaning, and the ס is for *sod*, the secret or Kabbalistic meaning. There is an additional, parallel structure of four levels of learning referred to by another acronym: טנתא. These four levels are from above to below. The ט is for *te'amim*, the musical notes denoting the way the Torah is chanted, the song of the Torah; the נ is for the *nekudot*, the vowels; the ת is for the *tagin*, the crowns upon certain letters; the א is for the *otiot*, the letters. The musical notes are considered the highest level of understanding, the song which reveals the deepest secrets of the letters themselves.

Until now we have merely traced the known qualities of music and song throughout human and Jewish history and describe their universal appeal and effect on body and soul, without fully understanding from where this unique power comes.

Here, though, we begin to touch upon the source of the mystical power of music. For the Divine creative process as expressed in the ten utterances and the ten *sefirot* produces what poets have called the harmony of the spheres. To be in tune with this celestial symphony is to be connected to the very fabric and pulse of creation, and herein lies the underlying power of music and its effect on the soul of man. For if God created the world through Divine speech and song, then it is this energy with which we come into contact with music.

When we sing we come into contact with a force much greater than ourselves. When we listen to music it resonates within us because — similar to prayer being not just something we do but something we are — music is not merely something we enjoy, but rather the essence of Divine creation and our own inner selves. Music opens us up to the myriad of physical and spiritual forces all around us, allowing us to become one with all creation and with its Source.

A Unified Universe

The giving of the Ten Commandments at Mount Sinai was accompanied by a number of natural and metaphysical phenomena: "And it came to pass on the third day in the morning that there was thundering and lightning and a thick cloud upon the mountain, and the sound of a shofar exceedingly loud..." (Exodus 19:16). Later it states: "And all the people saw the sounds of the thundering and the lightning and the sound of the shofar and the mountain smoking..." (ibid., 15). Rashi comments that all the people were able to see that which is heard, something which cannot ordinarily happen. This phenomenon is called synesthesia, a state where the senses are able to cross each other and one of the senses can comprehend another sense in a new way. The ability of all the people to see the sounds of the shofar represents a heightened state of consciousness, where the harmony of the spheres, the music of creation, is not only heard but seen.

The word for "smoking" [mountain] in Hebrew, עשן, is comprised of three letters, which form an acronym for the various dimensions of reality, as taught by the *Sefer Yetzirah* (3:3). The letter *ayin* (ע) represents *olam*, world or space; the letter *shin* (ש) represents *shanah*, year or time; the letter *nun* (נ) represents *nefesh*, soul, which is understood to be a moral and ethical dimension as real as the other, physical dimensions. Although Albert Einstein was able to reveal just one hundred years ago that time is also a dimension and that space and time form one unified continuum, science has yet to grasp soul as a "dimension."

It is explained in Kabbalah that as God uttered the Ten Commandments, the quintessential essence of Torah morals and ethics, all the dimensions of physical and spiritual reality were perceived by the people as one and unified. In fact, the Midrash tells us that at first God said all the Ten Commandments simultaneously, and only afterwards repeated them word by word (*Mechilta*, quoted in *Rashi* on Exodus 20:1).

The sentence introducing the Ten Commandments, "And God spoke all these things, saying," consists of twenty-eight letters and seven words, the exact number of letters and words in the first sentence of the Torah: "In the beginning God created the heavens and the earth." We are taught that the giving of the Torah represents the fulfillment of the purpose of the creation and that in fact all of creation was "on condition" that the Jewish people would accept the Torah at Mount Sinai (*Rashi* on Genesis 1:31).

The ten utterances of creation are thus transformed and revealed in a new form as the Ten Commandments. Just as God, as it were, "sang" the world into existence, so too were the Ten Commandments revealed, as it were, through Divine song. That is the symbolism of the sounds of the shofar growing exceedingly louder during the experience of receiving the Torah, which, as we have learned, is itself called song. It is as if the shofar acted as the background music for the Ten Commandments.

The thread connecting the Creator and the Torah, His Divine creative instrument, with all of creation is in essence music. God writes the musical score, the Torah, and gives it to man in order that we perceive the Divine symphony all around us. It is ultimately up to us, though, to decide whether we will learn the notes, hear the music, and become partners with God in enriching the harmony, or whether we will go about our business deaf to the beautiful tapestry of sound we call the universe.

The Song of Creation

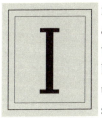n earlier chapters we discussed how the prayers and psalms often refer to joyous service of God through music, song, and praise. We brought but a few of the many examples of man being urged to exalt his Creator, in addition to descriptions of the angels and higher heavenly beings praising God daily.

Yet, according to the psalms of David, man and angel are not alone in giving thanks and lauding God; every creation, whether mineral, vegetable, or animal, is urged to express its joy at being part of the created universe:

> Praise [God], sun and moon; praise Him, all the shining stars. Praise Him, the most exalted of the heavens and the waters that are above the heavens....
>
> Praise God from the earth, sea giants and the watery depths. Fire and hail, snow and vapor, stormy wind fulfilling His word. Mountains and the hills, fruit trees and all cedars. Animals and all cattle, crawling things and winged birds....

> Let them praise the Name of God....
>
> (Psalms 148:1–6)

According to David not all the creations even need urging, for example:

> For the Conductor, a song of David. The heavens declare the glory of God, and the expanse of the sky tells of His handiwork....
>
> (Psalms 19:1–2)

> The hills are clothed with sheep, the valleys are covered with grain; they shout for joy, they sing.
>
> (Psalms 65:14)

On Shabbat morning the following words are recited from the beautiful song *Keil Adon* ("God the Master"):

> Good are the luminaries that our God has created,
> He has formed them with knowledge, understanding, and intelligence.
> Strength and power He has given them,
> To be rulers within the world.
> Filled with splendor and radiating brightness,
> Their splendor is beautiful in all the world.
> Glad as they go forth and happy when they return,
> They do with awe the will of their Creator.
> Beauty and glory they give His name,
> Joy and glad song at the mention of His kingdom....

In numerous places David sings that, in the future, when God is fully revealed in the world and His kingdom is accepted by one and all, all of creation will rejoice in His rule. Some of these psalms are recited on Friday night as we greet the Shabbat. In general, Shabbat is a time of heightened sensitivity to spiritual forces, a time to experience the inner dimensions of reality and the future Messianic era already in the present:

> Declare among the peoples, "God reigns." Indeed the world is established so that it cannot falter. He will judge the peoples with fairness. The heavens will be glad and the earth will rejoice, the sea and its fullness will roar; the field and everything in it will exult. Then all the trees of the forest will sing with joy before God, for He will have arrived, He will have arrived to judge the earth. He will judge the world with righteousness and the people with truth.
>
> (Psalms 96:10–13)

> Call out to God, all the inhabitants of the earth; open your mouths in joyous song and play music. Play music to God on a harp, with harp and the sound of chanted praise. With trumpets and the shofar sound, call out before God the King. The sea and its fullness will roar, the world and those that dwell in it. Rivers will clap hands, mountains will exalt together before God, for He will have come to judge the earth.
>
> (Psalms 98:4–9)

Previously we questioned whether to understand the notion of Divine speech creating the world as literal or figurative. We can ask the same question here. How should we interpret the above examples of the myriad elements of creation having the ability and consciousness to sing? It certainly would be easy to view the descriptions of inanimate matter, vegetation, and animals praising and singing to God as mere poetic license or flights of fancy. Yet perhaps there is a deeper layer of reality being revealed to us by David, the "sweet singer of Israel."

The Songs of Perek Shirah

The idea that every creation has a special song that it sings forms the basis of an intriguing and mysterious *midrash* called Perek Shirah, literally translated as "Chapter of Song." In this short and concise text, different creations sing specific verses from the Torah. Why each creation sings its particular verse is not explained, though many of the explanations are obvious. A few examples are:

> The palm is saying: "The righteous flourish like the palm tree; they grow like the cedar of Lebanon" [Psalms 92:13].
>
> The seas are saying: "More than the voices of many waters, than the mighty waves of the sea, God on high is mighty" [Psalms 98:8].
>
> The moon is saying: "He made the moon for the festivals; the sun knows the time of its coming" [Psalms 104:19].
>
> The ant is saying: "Go to the ant, you sluggard; consider her ways and be wise" [Proverbs 6:6].
>
> Many other creations sing verses which on first glance do not

connect to them at all, leaving us to contemplate why those particular verses are theirs.

The authorship of *Perek Shirah* has not been absolutely established, although according to many traditions it was written by King David, either alone or with his son Solomon, whom the Bible calls the wisest of men (Kings I 5:11). Others attribute it to one of the sages of the Mishnah, who lived approximately two thousand years ago.

There are a number of Kabbalistic texts whose teachings were handed down in secret manuscripts or by oral transmission over many generations until they were recorded and revealed to the wider public. This may be the situation here as well. In all cases, it seems clear that the inspiration and spirit of *Perek Shirah* was King David and his example of attributing song to all creation.

Perek Shirah consists of six chapters, each of which focuses on a different group of creations. The first chapter relates in general the songs of the earth: the wilderness and fields, the seas, wellsprings and rivers. The second chapter describes the songs of the elements of the heavens: day and night, sun, moon, and stars, clouds, lightning, rain, and dew. The third chapter is devoted to the songs of the vegetable kingdom: a variety of trees and the vine, wheat and barley, vegetables and grasses. The fourth chapter gives voice to the songs of numerous different birds and fish. The fifth chapter highlights the songs of the animals, both wild and domesticated. The sixth and last chapter enumerates the songs of the creeping creatures.

From the tiny ant to the kingly lion, from soaring birds to fish of the great depths, from lowly grasses to the towering palm tree, from wispy clouds to drops of rain, from lightning bolts to the distant stars, each and every creation has its song. We will now delve deeper into this most intriguing and enigmatic concept in order to understand what it means that each creation has its own song.

The Singers of Perek Shirah*

The first question asked by commentators down the ages is who exactly is singing the songs attributed to each creation. Four basic answers are given, each one true from its own perspective. Thus, the four answers are not in contradiction with each other, but rather they ultimately complement each other.

The first opinion given by a minority of commentators is that the creation itself sings the song attributed to it. The implication is that even inanimate objects have some sort of life force and consciousness that enables them to sing. Maimonides, in the beginning of his classic work, the *Mishneh Torah*, states that although the lower elements of fire, earth, air, and water do not have consciousness, the stars and planets do. They recognize their Creator and are aware of their own existence and therefore sing praises to God, as do the angels (*Mishneh Torah, Hilchos Yesodei HaTorah* 3:9–10).

The Arizal, the famous Kabbalist of Safed in the 1500s, taught that all four levels of creation — inanimate, vegetable, animal, and human — all have life force and consciousness, albeit on very different levels. All manifestations of reality are animated by a spark of God, and in this sense every point of creation has life force.

---

* The ideas presented in the rest of this section (through page 78) were taught by Rabbi Yitzchak Ginsburgh, based on Kabbalistic and Chassidic sources.

Therefore, we can understand that the creations themselves are singing their particular song with whatever level of consciousness they have.

This view is substantiated by the Midrashic view of the following description of the wisdom of King Solomon: "And he spoke three thousand proverbs and his songs were a thousand and five. And he spoke of trees, from the cedar tree that is in Lebanon to the hyssop that comes out of the wall; he spoke also of beasts and of birds, and of creeping things and of fishes" (Kings I 5:12–13). Some commentators explain from these verses that Solomon knew the healing properties of trees, plants, and herbs and the essential properties of all animals. Other commentators, based on various Midrashic traditions, interpret the words "he spoke of" to mean "he spoke *with*" trees, plants and herbs as well as the animals, understanding their language and communicating with them.

There are many other Jewish sources that describe animals, vegetation, and even inanimate objects speaking and communicating with man.

The second opinion is that an angel or a directing spiritual force from above sings the song of each creation listed in *Perek Shirah*. The fact that every creation has a guiding angel is stated in the Talmud: "No blade of grass grows until its [guiding] angel above strikes it and says, 'Grow' " (*Bereishit Rabbah* 10). In addition to every blade of grass having a corresponding angel above, we are taught that all grasses together have an angel or animating spiritual force who helps direct their development. This is true of all the specific and collective forms, species, and orders of creation. Each physical creation is considered to have a corresponding spiritual form above, the animating root force from which it is sustained in this world.

We are similarly taught that each person has his or her particular guiding angel. On the biblical story of Jacob fighting with "a man," Rashi comments that the adversary was actually the angel of Esau. As the morning came and the angel saw he could not defeat Jacob he said: "Let me go for it is dawn" (Genesis 32:27). Rashi, based on the Talmud, comments that the reason the angel desired to leave just then was that he needed to return to his heavenly abode to sing praises to God.

Each nation as well has one guardian angel who helps direct its affairs from the upper worlds. One biblical example of this is in the story of the Exodus. After letting the Jews leave Egypt Pharaoh had a change of heart. He gathered his armies and gave chase: "Pharaoh approached; the children of Israel lifted up their eyes and behold Egypt was journeying after them and they were frightened…" (Exodus 14:10). Because the verse uses the singular word *Egypt* rather than the plural *Egyptians*, Rashi quotes the Midrash that says they beheld the guardian angel of Egypt coming from Heaven to assist them.

According to this opinion, the inner motivational life force, the root form above, or the guiding angel is the one singing the song of each creation.

The third opinion is that it is neither creation nor angel but man himself who is singing in *Perek Shirah*. As man observes the world he lives in he learns various lessons from the workings of heaven and earth, the cycles of nature, and the plethora of living creatures who inhabit our planet. Enlightenment and insight can come from observing a falling leaf, an ant colony busy at work, the ever-changing shapes of the clouds, spring flowers in full bloom, a bubbling brook, a bird building her nest, a tree standing dormant in the snow, or a sunset over the ocean. We interpret the world around us, integrate it, and are inspired by it, and these insights and deep connections are translated into the various songs of the creations.

It is stated in the Talmud in the name of Rabbi Yochanan that had the Torah not been given we would have learned modesty from the cat, the prohibition of theft from the ant, the prohibition of forbidden relationships from the dove, and the way of proper marital relations from the fowl (Eruvin 100b). The idea of learning from all of creation is an extension of another dictum by the Sages: "Who is the wise one? One who learns from every person" (Pirkei Avot 4:1). This worldview sees life as the greatest teacher. As one learns from everyone and everything, this helps create a nullification of ego sufficient to grasp the inner essence of all things. That realization is then expressed as the song of that creation.

When Adam was first placed in the Garden of Eden, the Torah relates that God brought all the animals to him to see what he would name them, "and whatever Adam called it, that was its name" (Genesis 2:19). It is explained in Kabbalah that Adam, upon deep contemplation, was able to intuit the essence of each animal and thereby choose the exact Hebrew letters that would best convey that essence, and "that was its name." The process of giving names to all the animals is similar to recognizing which song each creature sings.

The fourth opinion is that God Himself is singing the song of each creation. According to the idea that God "sings" the world into creation, that original energy of song exists in each and every point of reality. Alternatively, it is the *Shechinah*, the Divine Presence, dwelling within each creation that is singing through it.

We are taught that the *Shechinah* spoke through the throat of Moses (Tikunei Zohar 38). When Moses, due to his great humbleness, first objected to being chosen the leader especially because of his inability to speak, God replied: "Who has made man's mouth or who makes a man mute, or deaf, or seeing, or blind? Is it not I, God? Now go and I will be with your mouth and will teach you what to say" (Exodus 4:11–12). God is, as it were, the "mouth" or song of every creation.

Each of these four opinions contains an element of truth and all together complement each other, providing a deep understanding of how different levels of truth and reality interconnect and ultimately fuse together in a perfect unity.

The Four Ascending Levels of Prayer

The four views on the songs of *Perek Shirah* further correspond in a most beautiful manner to the order of our daily morning prayers, which can be perceived as four ascending levels.

The first major section of the prayers, after the preliminary morning blessings, is *Pesukei DeZimrah*, verses of song. These verses are replete with references to the song and praise of the natural world, as discussed in chapter two. This section of prayer corresponds to the notion that each creation itself sings its song in *Perek Shirah*. It is interesting to note that, according to Kabbalah, before the Sages established the current order of the prayers, *Perek Shirah* filled the role of *Pesukei DeZimrah* in arousing human consciousness to praise of God.

Next in the order of the prayers is the section of blessings preceding the Shema, the Torah's cardinal statement of faith in One God. This section describes in majestic language how the angels and various heavenly beings daily praise God from on high. This corresponds to the second view that the angel of each creation sings in *Perek Shirah*.

The Shema, the third level of prayer, is considered the song of man. Thus, it corresponds to the idea that man is singing the song of creation. The first verse of the Shema is "Hear, O Israel, the Lord is our God, the Lord is one" (Deuteronomy 6:4). This is interpreted to mean "Know [or understand] that God is one," and by extension, that all reality is ultimately united in His essential oneness. By coming to know and understand the unity of God and His creation, man acquires the ability to hear the song of creation and to express its essence through his own song.

The Shema is followed by the *Amidah*, the silent prayer, where man directly approaches God and pours out his heart. After the *Amidah* is the section of prayer called *Tachanun*, consisting of confession and a plea for God's compassion. Here we recite the thirteen attributes of compassion as taught by God to Moses after the sin of the golden calf. The Talmud relates that God, as it were, covered Himself with a tallit, a prayer shawl, and taught Moses the Divine formula for eliciting compassion. This formula can be viewed as God's song and prayer and corresponds to the fourth view that it is God who sings in *Perek Shirah*.

Each of the four levels of song in the morning prayers has one verse that epitomizes the entire section. In *Pesukei DeZimrah*, the song of the creation, it is the final verse of Psalms: "Let all souls praise God, Halleluyah!" (Psalms 150:6). [This verse can also be translated as "Let everything that has breath praise God, Halleluyah!" or "Let the entire soul praise God, Halleluyah!"] As the concluding verse it is the "seal" of all the psalms and the climactic expression of the aspiration of the soul to serve God.

As mentioned above, the Arizal taught that every creation has some level of soul and consciousness. This verse, with its description of all of creation praising and singing to God, can be understood as the aspiration of not just the human soul to serve God, but also of each and every creation to do so. After this verse, we say, "You have made heaven, the most exalted heaven and all their legions, the earth and everything upon it, the seas and everything in them, and You give them all life…" (Nehemiah 9:6). Here we see that even the inanimate is considered to have "life" on some level.

The song of the angels, recorded in the book of Isaiah, is placed in the middle of the blessing preceding the Shema: "Holy, holy, holy is God, the Lord of Hosts; the whole world is filled with His glory" (Isaiah 6:3). This verse is sung every day by the angels and heavenly beings in great awe, tranquility, and sweetness.

The central song of man in prayer is clearly the Shema: "Hear, O Israel, the Lord is our God, the Lord is one." Here Israel represents the ideal man, while the Shema articulates the mission of the Jewish people to bring all mankind to recognize and worship God as one.

The song of God is the thirteen attributes of mercy. It is interesting to note that the thirteen attributes of mercy are considered so holy that they can only be recited in a minyan, a prayer quorum. Yet an individual may recite them if he or she does so with the musical cantillation of the Torah reading.

The initial letters of the first words of each of the four cardinal verses brought above can be arranged to spell the word אשקך, which has two possible meanings: "I would kiss you" and "I would cause you *to drink*." Amazingly, both meanings come in two consecutive verses in the Song of Songs: "When I should find you outside I *would kiss you* and none would scorn me. I would lead you and bring you to the house of my mother who brought me up; I *would cause you to drink* of spiced wine, of the juice of my pomegranate" (Song of Songs 8:1–2).

The idea of kissing and drinking wine are actually mentioned together at the very beginning of the Song of Songs: "The song of songs which is by Solomon. Let him kiss me with the kisses of his mouth, for your love is better than wine." The numerical value of *yayin*, wine, in Hebrew is seventy, the same as the value of *sod*, which means "secret." The commentators therefore explain, "Let him kiss me with the kisses of his mouth" to mean that Israel longs for closeness with God, through God communicating His deepest secrets of the Torah. That experience is greater than any physical gratification or stimuli the world can offer.

Kissing and song are similar in that they both express something that is impossible for words to do alone. The word אשקך, "I would kiss you," alluding to the four levels of prayer, is the song of all strata of creation in a state of existential prayer, longing for intimate closeness with God. Prayer on this level expresses the passion of the soul, and in essence all creation, to be united with God.

The word "kissing" is mentioned exactly thirteen times in the five books of Moses, the same number as the attributes of mercy. God's mercy is, as it were, His way of kissing man.

The "kisses of his mouth" is associated with *ta'amei hamitzvot*, the deeper, secret reasons of the mitzvot, which are to be revealed by the Messiah. The word *ta'am* (the nonconjunctive form of *ta'amei*) is also used for the musical cantillations of the Torah, the highest level of understanding, as discussed above. The Messiah will reveal the deepest levels of Torah understanding as the full expression of the song of the Torah. The tenth and consummate song of history — to be sung by the exiles as they come back to Israel — will harmonize perfectly with the highest levels of understanding reality that will be taught by the Messiah.

The Connection to the Ten Sefirot

The four levels of prayer and the four views of the singers in *Perek Shirah* have a further connection to the number ten, which as we have seen is an intrinsic link between many different aspects of song. The number ten is associated with four progressing levels of song: 1) *shir pashut*, singular song (the song of God); 2) *shir kaful*, a double song (the song of man); 3) *shir meshulash*, triple song (the song of the angels); and 4) *shir meruba*, quadruple song (the song of creation). These four levels create a triangle of ten points:

•
• •
• • •
• • • •

These ten points as they appear in the triangle connect to one of the most important ways of envisioning the ten *sefirot*. The singular song refers to *keter*, the crown, associated with the oneness and kingship of God. The double song refers to *chochmah* and *binah*, wisdom and understanding, which are called "two companions who never separate." The triple song refers to *chesed*, *gevurah*, and *tiferet*, mercy, judgment, and compassion, the three cardinal attributes of the heart. The quadruple song refers to *netzach*, *hod*, *yesod*, and *malchut*, eternity, glory, foundation, and kingship, which relate to the more behavioral, instinctive levels of the psyche. Understanding this structure of the ten *sefirot* as representing four levels of song further strengthens the concept that song lies at the essence of the Divine creative process, inasmuch as the ten *sefirot* are essentially connected with the ten statements through which God sang the world into existence.

There is a very important concept in Kabbalah called "run and return." This phrase is used by Ezekiel to describe the movement of certain angels he saw in his vision of the Divine chariot: "And the living creatures ran and returned like the appearance of lightning" (Ezekiel 1:14). The concept of "run and return" represents the basic movement of all life, whether physical, psychological, or spiritual. It is the throbbing pulse of blood, the beating of the heart, and the dual motion of our every breath. It manifests in the mystery of repeating cycles of the seasons and of nature. It is the dynamic of our ever-changing emotions and roller-coaster mood swings, feeling sometimes close to God and others, and at other times as far away as can be. It is the very pulse of life.

The song of each creation is the expression of its life force, its constant dynamic pulse. That which "moves" is alive, and if it is alive its life force is ultimately expressed in song. Even the inanimate "moves." Its physical essence is a whirling, frenetic combination of atoms and molecules; though it appears to be still, or, in the language of Kabbalah, "silent," its very essence is in fact movement. It may seem to be silent now, but in the future we are told that "a stone from a wall will cry out" (Habakkuk 2:11).

Each creation singing its unique song is a reflection of the Divine spark animating it and giving it life. It is the manifestation of music being not something we do, but what we are.

Music and Science

 p to this point, we have examined the strands of music and song as they weave themselves through creation and Jewish history, as well as music's essential connection to Torah, prayer, meditation, and spiritual experience. We will now examine whether these concepts and traditions are also substantiated by scientific findings.

Before delving into this subject it should be noted that in essence the Torah does not look to science or any other secular knowledge for validation. Truth exists on many levels, and the truth of Torah stands independent of scientific scrutiny. If this is so, then why try to bridge Torah and science?

The answer to this is ingrained in Torah wisdom and worldview. Judaism by nature seeks the revelation of unity in the world, from the oneness of God to the ultimate interconnectedness of all His creation (Rabbi Yitzchak Ginsburgh, *Living in Divine Space* [Jerusalem: Gal Einai, 2003], pp. 43–44). Torah plants this idea in all aspects of life, from the practical to the mystical. It is natural then to seek to find a common language between secular disciplines and the wisdom of the Torah. In fact, all knowledge and wisdom have their ultimate source in Torah, as is stated: "Turn it and turn it, for all is in it [Torah]" (*Pirkei Avot* 5:26).

Our Sages and rabbis throughout the ages have recognized the importance of examining the physical world to further Torah knowledge, and there is a wealth of writings on this subject. Many of our greatest rabbis displayed thorough knowledge of medicine, mathematics, astronomy, linguistics, music, philosophy, psychology, and agriculture. One just has to learn Talmud to get a sense of how well rounded and knowledgeable our Sages truly were.

Maimonides (1135–1204) in his day urged the study of the natural sciences as a way to come to appreciate the wonders of creation and the infinite wisdom of the Creator. Rabbi Bahya ibn Pakuda (1050–1120), in his great work *Duties of the Heart*, advocated the study of nature and other aspects of the physical universe (*Duties of the Heart* [New York: Feldheim Publishers, 1970], p. 133). Rabbi Judah Loew, the Maharal of Prague (1525–1609), wrote the following: "A man ought to study everything that will enable him to understand the essential nature of the world. One is obligated to do so, for everything is God's work. One should understand it all and through it recognize one's Creator" (*Writings of the Maharal of Prague* [Jerusalem: Mossad Harav Kook, 1960], vol. 2, p. 120). The Vilna Gaon (1720–1797), one of the greatest scholars of the last thousand years, was a great supporter of studying all the arts and sciences. He especially mentions the benefits of studying music, stressing its quality of bringing about spiritual elevation and a state of ecstasy, as well as the fact that it is instrumental to understanding the cantillation of the Torah. (See Rabbi Berel Wein, *Triumph of Survival: The Story of the Jews in the Modern Era* [New York: Mesorah Publications, 1990], p. 107.)

Music and Science • 83

In our day there is a great thrust towards understanding secular knowledge in light of the Torah, and merely by visiting a Jewish book store one can see how many books already exist combining the cutting edge of science, cosmology, quantum physics, psychology, medicine, environment, and more with Torah wisdom. Often these books relate especially to Kabbalah, whose metaphysical concepts are seen by more and more people as having great relevance to our contemporary world.

Therefore, in seeking a common language with science, we are not looking for validation of the Torah viewpoint but rather seeking to reveal new and valuable insight into the nature of reality. The deeper our understanding of the sciences and the arts, the richer our concept of Torah becomes. The more Torah we learn, the broader our appreciation for the laws and aesthetics of nature. The goal in many cases is to simply show that what at first seems like two different worldviews is in truth two different descriptions of the same ideas and phenomena.

Scientific Fact and the Sefirot

Let us return to the questions at hand. Is there some scientific explanation that parallels and helps explain the concept of music infusing all creation, and how can we understand from a scientific point of view each creation having its own unique song?

Firstly, it should be noted that the idea of Torah as the blueprint of creation, the *sefirot* as a Divine model manifesting itself throughout the physical and spiritual worlds, and the Hebrew letters as the building blocks of all existence are mirrored in various explanations of the laws of nature. Just as a scientist would describe atoms, molecules, and elements as the building blocks of creation and the "stuff" underlying all physical reality, the Torah uses the concept of the letters. Each letter is a channel of Divine influx and creative energy. To say an entity is created, maintained, and identified by its letter combinations is parallel to saying something is what it is due to its atomic and molecular makeup.

Similar to how we see the entire DNA code appearing in virtually every cell of the body, Kabbalah describes the *sefirot* as existing in all manifestations of time and space. The concept of Torah as the blueprint of creation resembles the varied laws of nature that give order and a sense of form and recognizable pattern to the universe.

Rabbi Yitzchak Ginsburgh, a great contemporary proponent of paralleling all secular sciences and arts to the wisdom of Torah, explains that the secret codes of nature, such as DNA, are similar to the musical notes which every component of creation sings as it plays its part in the cosmic symphony (Rabbi Yitzchak Ginsburgh: *The Hebrew Letters: Channels of Creative Consciousness* [Jerusalem: Gal Einai, 1990], p. 331).

The concept of music being at the very core of creation and of God speaking, or singing, the world into being can be seen from how music manifests itself. Music at its most fundamental level consists of sound waves formed by various vibrations and frequencies emanating from a musical instrument or from our vocal chords. One can feel these vibrations by putting his hand on his throat when speaking and see them in the vibrating strings of a guitar.

The concept of waves, vibrations, and frequencies applies on an even deeper level than this when we look into the nature of material reality. Electromagnetic energy, one of the four basic forces of the universe, as we now know, consists of waves. The intensity of a frequency determines whether it will manifest as light, X rays, gamma rays, microwaves, infrared, or ultraviolet. Light acts as both wave and particle, which is one of the greatest paradoxes and mysteries of modern science.

It has now been shown that all matter in fact consists of waves, albeit on the microscopic quantum level. The famous $E=MC^2$ equation by Einstein, which forever changed our perception of the physical universe, revealed the intrinsic connection between energy and matter. The fact that all energy and matter consists of waves leads us to understand much better the concept of God singing the world into existence and the "music of the spheres" as an extremely appropriate description.

It is no longer mystics and poets alone who speak of the intrinsic connection between music and creation. Scientists themselves, including many of the greatest living physicists, are discussing it. Paul Davies in his book *Other Worlds* describes how atoms and their subatomic particles can be compared to organ pipes which produce sound only according to certain well-defined notes that fit the geometry of the shape of the pipes. So, too, each atom is characterized according to its energy vibration or frequency, which he calls "subatomic music" (*Other Worlds* [New York: Simon and Schuster, 1980]).

He goes on to further explain that though the wave nature of quantum matter may seem different at first from the production of musical notes, these phenomena are in fact one and the same. The spectrum of light emanating from an atom is similar to the pattern of sound produced by a musical instrument. Just as each instrument has its own sound, so too the light emanating from atoms differs according to each atom's internal vibration. This insight helps us understand how at Mount Sinai we saw the sounds and heard the sights — for in essence they are both waves!

String Theory

Although the intrinsic connection between the inner workings of the atom and music has been scientifically accepted, it has received even more emphasis recently due to "string theory," which attempts to explain exactly how the "music" of the atom is produced. String theory posits that the smallest components of all atomic particles are not points, but vibrating strings whose different patterns of vibration produce the mass and the force charge of the atom. Brian Greene, in his now classic work *The Elegant Universe* (New York: Random House, 1999), explains how the observed property of fundamental particles of an atom are the result of the internal strings' particular pattern of vibration. He too remarks that the metaphor of music for the harmony of nature has taken on a truly startling reality.

If these ideas of string theory are not amazing enough, the theory has a number of other elements that bear directly upon other aspects of music and creation that we have discussed throughout this book. The first is the idea that there are actually ten dimensions, not just the four dimensions of space-time that make up our perceptible world, but an additional six dimensions so small that they are "curled up" and as yet undiscovered. The idea of ten dimensions of reality is of course connected to the idea of the ten *sefirot*, the ten sayings through which the world was created, the ten songs of history, and the Ten Commandments. As we have seen, the number ten is used throughout Torah as a basic model and blueprint of existence.

Very recently string theory, due to a number of unsolved difficulties, added the possibility of an eleventh uniting dimension as well. This idea is also quite interesting in that when one studies the *sefirot* one learns that in truth there are eleven *sefirot*, but we only count ten of them to conform to the statement in the *Sefer Yetzirah* (1:4): "Ten and not eleven, ten and not nine." (When the *sefirah* of *keter*, crown, appears in the model of the ten *sefirot*, the *sefirah* of *daat*, knowledge, is not counted, and when *daat* is counted, *keter* is not.)

The reason why string theory came to theorize a universe of ten dimensions lies behind perhaps an even more fundamental connection between music and the structure of our world. From the time that Albert Einstein revealed the unity of matter and energy, he turned his attention to finding the scientific equation and understanding that would unite all the forces of the universe. Though he was not able to accomplish this, the quest for the unified field theory, or the "theory of everything," has been adopted by the entire scientific world.

Unity in the Forces of the Universe

The concept that all the forces of the universe must somehow be united is not a new idea. Jewish belief in the unity and oneness of God includes the notion that in essence all manifestations of physical and spiritual reality are one, in that they all emanate from the one God. It is highly significant that the essential name of God has four letters, the same number as the basic forces of the universe: gravity, electromagnetism, the strong nuclear force, and the weak nuclear force. String theory holds the possibility that these forces are united by the vibrating strings at the very foundation of all reality. Through the perfection of the theory, an equation may be formulated which will show how these four forces are essentially united and ultimately how to use this understanding. (One of the alternative versions of string theory posits twenty-six dimensions, the numerical value of the four-letter name of God!)

The idea of unity relates to music in a very fundamental way. There is a big difference between noise and music. Noise is a haphazard or unpleasant combination of sound. Music implies order, harmony, symmetry, and beauty. The Torah metaphor of music in relation to the creation is born from the belief that there is an order, harmony, and purpose to creation. The cycles and laws of nature are not coincidental, rather the result of a Creator and a purpose. Music itself has an integral sense of order and symmetry. The symphony of creation is truly like an orchestra of widely different and unique instruments and musicians, all working together to make the most beautiful music. As an orchestra has a conductor whose job is to make sure all work together towards the same purpose, the universe has a Divine conductor orchestrating the whole production.

The particular qualities we identified in music, and especially in the ten songs sung throughout history, were the all encompassing attributes of purpose, unity, completion, and peace. Song in its truest sense reveals within a person a complete unity of body and soul, a sense of peace and completion that touches the deepest aspect of one's being.

The human psyche is an incredibly complex structure made up of countless different intellectual, emotional, and physical energies. As music produced by strings is seen as engraved in the very makeup of the physical universe and creating a virtual worldwide web of unity, so too music in the soul brings together all the different sides of a human being in order to achieve true unity and a symphony of ultimate purpose.

The quest for the unified field theory was stymied for years due to a critical problem. Einstein's theory of general relativity, its implications for how we see space-time, and its revolutionary revelations as to the workings of gravity created a new understanding of the order inherent in the bigger picture of the universe. Yet within just a few years quantum mechanics and the uncertainty principle revealed the inherent chaotic and unpredictable nature of the subatomic world. Einstein's objections to the initial revelations of quantum physics were summed up in his famous statement, "God does not play dice with the universe." Paradoxically, both theories have been proven to be true, though they stand in seeming contradiction one to the other.

Until quantum mechanics there was a growing belief in the deterministic nature of the universe. The laws of science were deemed to be so predictable that theoretically the future could be predicted if one knew all factors involved. Einstein's discoveries gave support to that idea. Along came quantum physics and proved that, at least on a subatomic level, nothing was actually predictable. The best we could achieve were approximate predictions of how subatomic matter would act. It turns out that the bigger picture of science shows immutable order, while the smaller picture reveals a teeming world of unpredictability and chaos.

This paradox parallels the age-old question of free will and determinism, which the Torah acknowledges and deals with in countless ways. Einstein's worldview was basically deterministic, while quantum mechanics conceptually allows the possibility of free will. This dilemma of science and philosophy is considered by the Torah as one of the greatest paradoxes of existence. Yet herein lies a great secret. Torah thought is not frightened by paradox; rather it embraces paradoxes and accepts the fact that paradoxes of all sorts exist at every level of reality. The paradox of light being both a particle and a wave, and general relativity and quantum mechanics both being true, are examples of paradoxes in the world of science. Man's ability to choose freely and God's knowledge of the future is also such a paradox. The Torah view that free will and God's providence are both true simultaneously is similar to the scientific view that both general relativity and quantum mechanics are true and operate concurrently.

We discussed previously the idea of the singers in *Perek Shirah* being the guiding angel of each creation. We learned that there is an angel guiding an entire order or species and in addition there are individual angels for each individual creation. It could be understood that there is a guiding force on the macrolevel of creation, as represented by the obvious order inherent in the laws and cycles of nature, yet each creation on the microlevel has a certain measure of independence and uniqueness called free will, or its own particular song, as represented by the unpredictability inherent in the microworlds.

The DNA code is not totally deterministic; rather, it forms the parameters within which choice and various possibilities operate. Just as each atom is vibrating according to its internal sense of music, so too every entity, from the smallest elements of creation to the largest, has its own song, its unique vibrational field. Each creation plays its part in the bigger picture of order and purpose infused in all existence.

In scientific terms this means that although general relativity and quantum mechanics seem to be in contradiction, this is not necessarily true. We can conceive of a greater surrounding sense of order permeating all creation, as well as the possibility of movement and adaptability. Though highly paradoxical, it can be understood that they both operate simultaneously and both are true. To find the unified field theory this paradox will have to be resolved, which is what string theory hopes to achieve.

Even if string theory cannot be proven, due to the fact that there are as yet no experiments that can actually observe the minuscule strings predicted, the connection between the metaphor of music and the created universe is already well established. String theory only attempts to show the overall unity of all things and how the music of the atom actually occurs.

The Music of the Animal Kingdom

On the scientific level, how can we understand that the animal, vegetable, and mineral kingdoms are singing? Although we discussed how the song of every creation and creature represents its actual physical nature, its unique vibrational essence, there is an additional theory that along with song comes some level of consciousness, no matter how basic or primitive.

We will begin from the easiest to understand and the closest to the nature of man, the animal kingdom. It is clear that animals have a certain level of soul. The word *nefesh,* used for the lowest level of the soul in man, is used a number of times in describing the creation of sea animals and birds on the fifth day of creation, and land animals on the sixth day. Both land animals and man were in fact created on the same day, alluding to a deep connection between animal and man. The word *nefesh* is often translated conceptually as "animal soul" and relates to our basic drives of survival and physical pleasure.

It is also clear that animals communicate with each other and with man, expressing intellect and emotions in various ways. We are familiar with the wide variety of sounds animals make, and many times we can differentiate between a sound of warning or pain, hunger or greeting. Animals also exhibit various traits of society in the manner in which they organize their herds, flocks, and families.

Although man and animal both have the faculty of communication, the unique ability of man to communicate complex intellectual and analytical thoughts differentiates between them. In relating to the Torah description of the creation of man, Onkelos translates the words "and man became a living soul" as "and man became a speaking spirit" (Genesis 2:7). Animals communicate their physical needs and even basic emotions connected to survival and pleasure, while man, in addition to those needs, communicates profound philosophical, spiritual, and existential ideas.

In the animal world there is certainly much song, especially among birds, whose chirping and melodic song is manifest virtually everywhere, adding a sense of background music to our lives. How many mornings do we awake to the gentle sound of song birds perched in a nearby tree? How often do we watch a sunset to the sound of birds harmonizing together? Who has not stood on a beach by the ocean waves as seagulls and waterbirds call eerily in the distance, or reached the top of a mountain and heard the song of birds hidden in the clefts of the rock?

The sounds and songs of the animal world that we hear are not the only ones that exist. There are many that are above and below our range of hearing. For example, bats, porpoises, shrews, and some insects communicate in the ultrasonic range, while crocodiles, whales, and elephants communicate in the infrasonic range.

Many animals incorporate song into their mating rituals. Female elephants, for example, announce their readiness for mating with a song which can last up to half an hour. The song has a certain form and sequence that researchers can discern, leading them to describe it as a song.

It is recorded that King Solomon, the wisest of men, "spoke... of beasts and of birds, and of creeping things and of fishes" (Kings I 5:13). As mentioned above, some commentators explain that King Solomon knew the language of each creature and how to communicate with them.

The sounds and songs of the animal world fill our world, yet many people are oblivious to them or take them for granted. Once a year, we observe a beautiful custom that acknowledges our appreciation to the birds for their daily music. On Shabbat Shirah, the Shabbat on which we read the song of the sea, it is customary to take some bread crumbs outdoors and leave them for the birds. Two reasons are given. The primary reason is to show appreciation for the birds' eating manna put out by Datan and Abiram, thus foiling the plot to challenge Moses' leadership. The secondary reason is to acknowledge our deep debt of gratitude for the birds' wonderful songs throughout the year.

The Music of the Vegetable Kingdom

Can there be song and consciousness in the vegetable kingdom as well? Much research has been done on plants in order to understand how they grow and thrive. Amazingly enough scientists have found that plants react to music, sounds, and even emotion. Plants actually grow best to the sound of very mellow music. Harsh, loud music disturbs plants, causing them to grow significantly more slowly. When people talk to plants in quiet, loving ways greater growth is observed, whereas anger and yelling inhibit growth. It has been shown that music quickens the streaming of protoplasm, and electric impulses in the form of waves have been recorded emanating from plants. These experiments were tried on whole fields as well as houseplants and greenhouses. Many of them are recorded in *The Secret Life of Plants* by Peter Tompkins and Christopher Bird (New York: Harper and Row Publishers, 1973).

Even more revolutionary claims, yet to be proven conclusively, have been made regarding experiments carried out by hooking up plants to lie detector polygraphs and to galvanometers to record responses to various stimuli. In these tests plants were shown to be quite aware of everything happening to them and around them and reacted in kind.

Although we usually don't think in these terms, photosynthesis can be compared to a very spiritual level of consciousness, as plants turn the light of the sun into chlorophyll, a basic ingredient of their life and growth. Light in Judaism always symbolizes spirituality, purity, and Divinity. The idea of taking the light of God and transforming it into personal growth and renewal is a basic concept in Kabbalah and Chassidut. It forms the basic paradigm of the soul's mission in the world, whereby we are always looking for fallen sparks of light and holiness in order to transform them, and in so doing to rectify the world.

Similarly, we are taught that by eating we extract the Godly kernel of life force from the food and transform it into spirituality by using it to fulfill our purpose in the world. By eating fruits and vegetables, and even animals that live by grazing, we are actually incorporating and integrating the original light transformed by plants. This ability of plants to turn light into life force represents a very advanced state of consciousness, from which man has much to learn. Just as we can learn so much about life from animals, so too can we learn profound lessons of life from trees and grasses, herbs and grains, flowers and bushes. In fact, when the Torah commands us not to cut down fruit trees, it compares man to a tree of the field (Deuteronomy 20:19). Even more, the Torah itself is compared to a tree: "It is a tree of life for all those who grasp it" (Proverbs 3:18). Additionally, the *sefirot* are many times referred to and artistically depicted as a "tree of life."

Throughout the ages Jewish mystics, prophets, and Sages went out to nature to receive inspiration and the word of God. Our patriarchs and matriarchs were shepherds living close to the land. The Arizal, the great Kabbalist of Safed in the 1500s, gave most of his teachings over to his students out in nature, far from the confines of the city. The Baal Shem Tov spent many of his earlier years wandering through forests and mountains and in doing so set the example for many Chassidic masters after him.

Rebbe Nachman of Breslov, the great-grandson of the Baal Shem Tov, put great emphasis on going out to nature in order to commune with God. This custom has been carried on by his followers to this very day. The following teachings of Rebbe Nachman, based on a section from his classic work *Likutei Moharan* (Part II, *Torah* 63) and adapted into a modern song taught to most Israeli schoolchildren, describes how each herb and grass has its own special melody, which in turn makes up the melody of the shepherd:

> you should know
> that each and every shepherd
> has his own melody
>
> you should know
> that every herb and grass
> has its own melody
>
> from the song of the grasses
> they make up the melody
> of the shepherd
>
> how beautiful!
> how beautiful and pleasant
> when hearing their song
>
> it is very good
> to pray among them
> and with joy
> serve God

and from the song of the grasses
the heart is filled and longs

and when the heart
is filled with song
and yearns for the land of Israel
a great light
is drawn forth
from the holiness of the land

and from the song of the grasses
is created the melody of the heart

The Rebbe of Vitebsk, who moved to Israel with a few hundred of his followers in the late 1700s, once made a celebration. He told his students that the reason he was celebrating was that for years he had longed to hear the song of the land of Israel, but until that day he had never merited to hear it. He described how that morning he had gone out to nature, as was his custom, and for the first time he could hear the song of the trees and the melody of the flowers and grasses of the field.

As the wind blew through the harp of David at midnight, creating a pleasant melody which awoke him, so too does the wind blowing through the branches of a tree or the grasses and grains in a field create a beautiful melody. A leaf driven along the ground or a log crackling in the fire are notes in a great cosmic symphony.

Rebbe Nachman was once a guest in a home. All night he couldn't sleep. In the morning he asked his host about the bed he had slept in and was told it was brand new, made from a young tree cut for that purpose. Rebbe Nachman explained that the reason he could not sleep was that he had heard the young tree still crying over its premature death.

Although the song of the vegetable kingdom is subtle in comparison to that of man and animals, it is there for those sensitive and spiritual enough to hear.

The Music of the Mineral Kingdom

In Kabbalah, the inanimate is called "mute." Unlike plants, which do have the properties of life, growth, and renewal, as well as the ability to perpetuate themselves, inanimate creatures seem to have no sign of life. But this is far from the truth. The inner, hidden, molecular world of inanimate creations teems with frenetic motion. The Arizal revealed that even the inanimate have a level of soul and consciousness and that sometimes human souls are reincarnated as stones or other such minerals in order to experience that reality for the sake of rectification.

The question of whether this level of creation can have any sort of consciousness has been sharpened by the famous double slit test, which was used to establish that light is both a particle and a wave. Light was allowed to pass through slits onto a screen, with the amazing result that it did not act as a group of particles. Instead, individual photons mysteriously cooperated with each other in order to create a wave effect. It was as if the individual photons knew what other photons were doing and whether the other slit was open or closed, even if shot through the slits one photon at a time at various intervals of time. The results have baffled and amazed scientists till this day.

In another test, photons are shot in two opposite directions towards polarizers. If one polarizer allows the photon travelling towards it through, then the opposite one will as well, no matter how much space is between them. This and many other experiments have established the indeterminacy of the microworld and the possibility of free will. It also raises puzzling questions about the conscious nature and free will, as it were, of even an atom.

Although the inanimate is mute on a certain level, there is another dimension to it as well. Waves of the ocean rolling onto the shore, a bubbling brook, a clap of thunder, a howling wind, an avalanche, and a host of other phenomena reveal to us the sounds of the inanimate world. Experiments have recorded earthquakes and volcanoes and an entire range of sound from nature beyond what human beings can hear. Just as we see but a small part of the electromagnetic spectrum of light, similarly we only hear but a small part of the incredibly rich and complex song of creation.

These ideas of science can be applied to the verses we quoted from the psalms of David, which at first glance seemed whimsical or even simplistic. What science knows through experimentation and discovery, the mystic, or the wise, receives through revelation. This can help us understand how so much of what is being revealed in modern science was known to the ancients, albeit with a different symbolic language and frame of reference.

We now know that there are not just hundreds of billions of stars, but actually hundreds of billions of galaxies, each one larger than the mind can comprehend. King David states in one of his psalms: "He [God] counts the number of the stars, to all of them He assigns names" (Psalms 147:4). A name in Judaism implies a unique essence and a unique destiny. The fact that God calls each star by name teaches us that every star, every leaf, each and every snowflake is indeed special and individually crafted. How much more special is a human being, whose soul is "an actual part of God above."

In Torah terms, and now more and more in scientific language as well, music exists at every level of creation, from the atom to the Milky Way and beyond. The idea that every creation has a song says that each and every entity has its own unique vibrational pattern which defines who and what it is. The mystical power of music is accessible when we tune in to the infinite tones and harmonies all around us, seen and unseen, heard and unheard. Music plugs us into the very fabric of creation and the Divine creative force which is renewing itself at every moment. When we sing, the whole world sings. When we are quiet and still, we can let the waves rolling over us bring us in tune with the melody of creation. The beat of music is the beat of the universe, and this is why it draws and attracts us in such a deep way.

Finding One's Own Song

One of the most important methods of study, especially in Chassidic teachings, is to take what we learn and make it relevant to our own lives. Each story and teaching in the Torah is not a one-time event from the distant past; rather, it speaks to us today. As Rashi teaches (on Exodus 19:1), we must all see and experience the Torah as if it was given today. Even mitzvot that are not practiced in our day have eternal spiritual lessons for each person and every generation. The characters and events in the Torah are archetypal and are therefore manifest within our intellect, emotions, and psyche, as well as in the social and political happenings of every era.

In this light, each person needs to understand and make personally relevant the idea that all creations, on both a physical and spiritual level, have their own song and identity, their own unique vibrational field. This last section will examine how to better understand and identify one's own song and how to ultimately use it as a vehicle through which to express oneself.

The Spark of God Within

According to Kabbalah, there is no place devoid of God's presence. Every point of reality receives its existence and inner life force from the Divine spark of God within it. When describing the creation of man the Torah states: "And God formed man of the dust of the ground and breathed into his nostrils the breath of life and man became a living soul" (Genesis 2:7). The dust of the ground relates to the physical composition of man, whereas the soul comes from the "breath" of God. When one wishes to blow something up, like a balloon, he takes a deep breath from within before blowing outwards. Similarly, the soul of man emanates, as it were, from the very internal essence of God.

In our morning prayers each day we mention that God "in His goodness renews daily the works of creation." Kabbalah and Chassidut teach that re-creation is not just a daily occurrence, but actually occurs at every instant. Modern science now affirms that within the dynamic inner world of the atom, particles are bursting in and out of existence for a billionth of a billionth of a second. Physical reality is not static, but is being re-created constantly at the most fundamental levels of existence.

God spoke and is, in fact, still speaking the world into being. Divine speech, as we have seen, can also be conceived as God's song of creation. Since we, like all other creations, are animated and owe our very existence to God, it follows that at the highest level an individual's song is the realization of the Divine spark within. This song is the breath of God giving us life. In Hebrew the word for breath, *neshimah*, comes from the same root as the word for soul, *neshamah*. Our souls are the breath of God, the song He sings through our very being.

The third book of the Torah, Leviticus, begins with God calling Moses from the newly erected Tabernacle. It is explained in Chassidut that this calling is directed to each and every person, a call to come close to God, to form a personal relationship with the Creator of the universe. This calling is the background music and stage upon which our lives are played out. God is speaking to us and calling us through the events and circumstances of our lives. We create our own unique song by harmonizing with the melody and by filling in specific notes through free will. Thereby Divine Providence and free will harmonize to form both a steady beat and a solo improvisation.

This understanding that our inner song is the spark of God within can be seen to correspond to the viewpoint that it is God who is singing the song of *Perek Shirah*. It is an awareness that God, as it were, sings through us.

Each Person's Unique Mission

It is taught throughout Jewish tradition that each person has a unique soul and a unique mission in the world. No one can complete another person's task for him or her. We all have our special contribution to make, our own instrument to play in the cosmic symphony. Finding and understanding our unique song is identical to realizing our latent potential.

We mentioned previously that music corresponds to the *sefirah* of *keter*, crown, the highest of the *sefirot*, relating to the subconscious and superconscious aspects of the soul. According to Kabbalah, *keter* is composed of three inner dimensions: faith, pleasure, and will. Music relates to all three levels.

The source of faith in the soul is so hidden that it is referred to in the *Zohar* as "the unknowable head," or at times "the head that neither knows or is knowable" (*Zohar, Idra Zutra, Parashat HaAzinu*). Accessing this level of soul only comes through nullification of the ego to the point of experiencing true oneness with God. The more we make His will our will and subjugate our animal soul to the Divine soul within, the more we nurture faith in the soul. A beautiful allusion to this is found in the fact that Hebrew words אני, "I," and אין, "[the Divine] nothing," have the same letters. Music and song emanate from the soul when the finite ego becomes "nothing" and merges with its infinite Divine source, referred to as the *ein sof*.

Faith corresponds to the highest level of soul, called *yechidah*, the unique aspect of the soul that defines the singular essence of an individual. This level is where the soul and God "touch," as it were, the junction where man and God meet. Faith in the soul relates to our awareness of being rooted in the essence of God and how this influences our entire being. Though we are usually unconscious of the impact this level of soul has upon us, it actually forms the ultimate frame of reference and the motivational thrust of our lives. It is the background music that we usually ignore.

Faith and song are intrinsically connected, as can be seen in the following verses relating to the song of the sea: "And God saved Israel on that day from the hand of Egypt and Israel saw the Egyptians dead on the seashore. Israel saw the great hand that God inflicted upon Egypt, and the people feared God and they had faith in God and Moses, His servant. Then Moses and Israel sang this song to God…" (Exodus 14:30–15:1). By attaining faith and trust in God and Moses, the people were inspired to sing the song of the sea, one of the ten archetypal songs. The recognition of faith in the soul releases even the most hidden potential, whose most fitting expression is music and song.

Pleasure at the realm of *keter* refers to the awareness of one's hidden potential and ultimate mission in the world. The soul experiences great pleasure when it perceives that it is achieving its goals and purpose in life. When we work and complete a goal, large or small, the soul senses great satisfaction. Faith entails not just belief in God, but belief that God, as it were, believes in us as well. Divine pleasure in the soul relates to the feeling that God not only believes in us, but is also actively assisting us in achieving our mandate in life. We are put into this world in order to fulfill a mission and one's song represents the ability to direct one's actions according to his or her calling in life.

In addition, pleasure relates to the subconscious and superrational experience of Divine bliss and peace. Music most certainly touches the source of Divine pleasure in the soul, allowing it to access multilevels of experience simultaneously. Music opens the gates of intellectual, emotional, and instinctive self-expression, as it creates the eternal present, touching and activating the portals of our own potential longing to be expressed. This ability to identify one's purpose and mission in the world corresponds to the viewpoint that human beings are the ones singing in *Perek Shirah*.

Being in Tune with One's Mission

Will, the lowest head of *keter*, takes the levels of faith and pleasure and begins to craft strategies for their fulfillment. It is here that the power of song in the soul begins to develop and take its place upon the stage of life. It becomes the force to transform potential into actual, bringing the hidden subconscious into the light of day.

When we become aware of an inner spiritual rhythm, we have a gauge to know when we are in tune with our mission in life. If we are in tune, it is as if an angel above is striking us and saying "Grow!" When we are truly in tune with the Divine cosmic rhythm and our own higher spiritual natures, we are able to grow and dance to the music. If we act counter to God's will and our own spiritual advancement, then the recording begins to skip and cacophony results.

There is no artist, no matter how naturally gifted, who does not apply the dictum that practice makes perfect. This practice keeps us in touch with our higher selves, our guiding sense of destiny. The level where one engages himself in perfecting his song and actually performing it in the world corresponds to the viewpoint that an angel or higher spiritual form is singing the songs of *Perek Shirah*.

Resonance with the World

The final viewpoint, which was the first one discussed above, is that the various creations themselves are singing in *Perek Shirah*. This view corresponds to the animal soul of man and its innate desires and needs. Here too is found a deeply ingrained song. For the animal soul, though intrinsically connected to the body, is capable of being transformed by the higher levels of soul until it too can uplift even the most mundane and earthly desire.

We are taught in biology that each person has a circadian rhythm, an inner cadence and pattern of hormones that order our habits of eating, sleeping, and so on. Though many times we need to overcome our innate instincts and habits, especially when they are harmful to us or contrary to Torah, our bodies have a natural inner song and a rhythm that are best heeded. We walk with a certain gait, talk in a certain tone, sleep better in a certain position, and digest our food best under certain conditions. Each person is a world to himself and no two people resonate physically or spiritually the same way.

Another all-encompassing set of rhythms surrounding us is the cycles of nature: the seasons, the tides, the rotations of the sun and the moon. All of these surround us constantly, the repeating refrain of life and ultimately of death as well. The cycle of the year and especially the Jewish cycle of Shabbat and the holidays brings us in tune with an even higher Divine cycle that is manifest in our natural world. The way each person reacts to these internal and external rhythms creates his or her song, his resonance with the world.

The Direct Connection to God

When trying to understand who is singing in *Perek Shirah* we built a structure from the lowest level to the highest. Here we began with the highest and went to the lowest. This alludes to the statement, "Their end is embedded in the beginning and the beginning in the end" (*Sefer Yetzirah* 1:7). It is interesting to note that one of the meanings of the word for song, *shir*, is "circle." The repeating nature of music is, in fact, similar to a circle. Music combines and harmonizes all the various octaves of reality, connecting body and soul, man and God, physical and spiritual, finite and infinite, in one unifying circle.

One of the most important teachings of the Baal Shem Tov is that each Jew has within a Messianic spark. This spark relates to the innate, inner spark of Godliness and our potential leadership qualities within. The Jewish people were designated to be "a kingdom of priests and a holy nation" (Exodus 19:6), which is a reference to our mission to be a "light for the nations" (Isaiah 49:6).

The name Israel in Hebrew, ישראל, can be read ישר א-ל, "straight to God." This reflects the fundamental Jewish belief that each person has a direct relationship with the Creator. Feeling this direct, personal connection allows a person to access his or her Divine soul, the source of all inner potential.

When the letters of ישראל are rearranged they spell שיר א-ל, "the song of God." We can learn from this that the straightest and most direct way to connect to God is through song, which in Hebrew has the same numerical value as prayer. The intense and intimate nature of prayer bonds us with God, and, like song, it is the deepest expression of a person's most inner essence.

Israel being "a kingdom of priests and a holy nation" is synonymous with Israel being the "song of God," both relating to the Jewish people's role in fulfilling God's purpose of creation. A number of times in the Talmud Israel is referred to as a partner with God in bringing the world to its rectified state. God creates the world with song and the fundamental physical laws of nature reflect music at all strata of existence. The mission of Israel is to reveal the existence and the unity of God reflected in all reality. This is the secret of the tenth and last song waiting to be revealed.

Rabbi Yitzchak Ginsburgh teaches that when enough people have activated their own Messianic spark, a critical mass will be attained, which in turn will draw the reality of the Messiah into the world. In this sense the Messiah is not just the answer to our prayers for redemption; he is the revelation and consummation of our own spiritual service. For this to occur, though, there must be a critical mass of redemptive energy manifest in the world.

According to tradition, the Messiah, Mashiach, will be a king, warrior, teacher, and leader. A permutation of the letters of the word Mashiach, משיח, spells ישמח, "to rejoice," alluding to the secret of the charisma the Messiah will exude. Joy is contagious and activates deep empathy and identification. Mashiach will influence each person to draw from within himself his Godly soul, until it expresses itself in all its glory.

We are taught that Pesach, the holiday of freedom, can be read פה-סח, "the mouth that speaks." Rabbi Yitzchak Ginsburgh teaches that freedom, from a personal, spiritual point of view, is the ability to fully express oneself, while slavery is the frustration born of the inability to express oneself. Music in the soul is the uninhibited expression of freedom and redemption.

The Talmud relates that King Hezekiah had great messianic potential, so much so that God wanted to make him Mashiach. After God performed a great miracle for him by smiting the armies of Sennacherib who had surrounded Jerusalem, King Hezekiah did not sing a song in praise of the great miracle. Because he could not fully express the redemption of that moment through song, he was not appointed Mashiach (*Sanhedrin* 94a). In our own personal lives, in order to actualize our own messianic spark, we should strive to avoid King Hezekiah's mistake.

How Do We Find Our Inner Song?

Finding one's inner song and learning how to express it in the world is obviously not an easy task, nor are there any firm guidelines for how to accomplish it. Each person has his own path towards enlightenment and discovering God, and each person must come to it through his own effort. Nevertheless, there are a number of tried-and-true methods that can assist us in this arduous but worthwhile quest.

It is said that identifying a problem is half the solution and asking the right question is half the answer. The first step is simply being aware that each person has a unique mission and certain specific tasks he needs to accomplish. This mission is one's inner song and it contains the key to personal freedom and redemption. It is the secret to understanding life and reality. It is a resonating force in the soul that, when grasped, yields great inner peace, direction, and power.

But how many people live life in such a way as to find and fulfill that mission? How many people dedicate themselves to rectifying blemishes in character traits and personality? How many people work hard at fulfilling their potential, toiling to give and be their very best?

When Cain and Abel brought offerings to God, the offering of

Abel was chosen while the offering of Cain was rejected (Genesis 4:2–8). Even though it was actually Cain's idea to bring the offering, he brought from the second best, the leftovers, while Abel brought from the very best. Ultimately, all that God wants is that we should try our very best.

In the story of Joseph and his brothers, Jacob sends his ten sons down to Egypt for grain a second time with the following words: "If it must be so now, do this, take of the best fruits [*zemirot*] in the land in your vessels and carry down to the man a present…" (Genesis 43:11). The word for "best fruits" in the verse is *zemirot*, the same as one of the words for song! The best of each person, his best fruits, is expressed in his song, in being the best he can be.

Seeking Help through Prayer

Turning to God in heartfelt prayer and asking for direction and assistance in fulfilling His will is an important and potent method for coming into tune with our inner song. The act of prayer itself allows us to hear with an inner ear our unique song. Just as a *niggun* is a song without words, the song of the soul is music that is heard by no physical ear, a complex symphony without a sound. Yet the more we get in tune with the "sounds of silence," the more this song can take on real notes and rhythm.

A famous story told over in various ways relates to an illiterate young Jew who was in the synagogue of the Baal Shem Tov one Rosh HaShanah. He longed to express himself in prayer, but not knowing the words, he instead began playing his flute. The congregation was shocked, since it is forbidden to play music on the holiday, but the Baal Shem Tov revealed to them that the boy's heartfelt song was so genuine that it had pierced the heavens, nullifying an evil decree.

Each person develops certain inner tunes that express the varied waves of emotion and the cycles of the psyche. These are important signs of a healthy inner psychological balance. When praying, we develop chants and intonations unique to ourselves. Communities adopt certain melodies for key sections of prayer that form a bond of identification among the participants. Shabbat and holiday tunes have developed over the generations to express the different nuances of each part of the prayer services. These particular melodies elicit deep feelings and even mystical experiences, touching the very depths of the spirit of man.

Along with our formal prayers, Chassidut teaches the importance of informal prayer, where we formulate our own individual communications with God. In this realm we can, like King David, make prayer something we are, not what we do. In this way we can truly unify prayer and song till they are virtually the same.

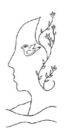

Reaching Our Song through Torah

Rebbe Nachman of Breslov taught that we need to turn our Torah into prayer and our prayers should be gleaned and studied for the Torah embedded in them. This is to say that our study should not be merely an intellectual pursuit, but we should constantly strive and pray to merit to fulfill the Torah we learn. Conversely, our prayers should not become so rote that we don't appreciate the multiple layers of meaning and intent infused in each word.

Since both prayer and Torah are intrinsically connected to music and song, it behooves us to bring more and more music into our prayers and into our Torah. This is true on both an individual and communal level. There is a great hunger in the world in general and in particular among the Jewish people today for authentic spiritual experience. Infusing prayer and Torah with music is to recapture and reveal an important component of spirituality for which the soul longs.

This theme was taught by the first generations of Chassidic masters, who all emphasized the importance of music for the individual and the community in the service of God. Since music itself helps one find his inner song, it is no surprise that the Chassidic movement produced so many great Rebbes, each one unique in his own way. To this day Chassidic Rebbes and teachers begin their classes with singing, and music is an integral part of virtually all Chassidic gatherings.

Meditation

Another important way to learn to hear one's inner song and the music inherent in the soul is through meditation. Jewish meditation has ancient roots and has been practiced by Sages and mystics throughout the ages, from Abraham down to our own day (See Rabbi Aryeh Kaplan's book, *Jewish Meditation* [New York: Schocken Books, 1985].) There are numerous forms of Jewish meditation, some similar to other types practiced in the world, while others, by far the majority, uniquely Jewish in content and form. It is an activity well worth practicing, for it is a very potent vehicle for getting in touch with the inner self and the Divine soul. Ultimately the goal of meditation is to connect with God, as well as to achieve new insight into life.

By quieting the mind and shutting out outer distractions and inner static, we begin to hear music on multiple levels: on the physical level, in the form of our heartbeat, the blood pulsing through our veins, and our steady breathing; in the vibrating energy in the matter all around us; in the longing of the soul to unite with its Creator and His song. The inner song and music of the soul can only be heard when we turn off the noise all around us and the constant monologue in our minds and tune into our essential self and its ultimate source in God.

Meditative practices can be combined with prayer, or with music, or by uniting all three activities together in such a way that each complements and strengthens the other. Meditation in Judaism is much more flexible than just sitting silently for a period of time. Jewish meditation takes many forms and can be practiced as a form of deep concentration and focus along with many of life's activities.

Meditation is particularly suited for studying Torah, as it says in the evening prayers: "We will discuss Your decrees and will rejoice with the words of Your Torah and with Your commandments for all eternity. For they are our life and the length of our days and about them we will meditate day and night." Meditating on the Torah we learn helps integrate the teachings in a way that makes them a real part of our inner consciousness.

The infinite essence and will of God is revealed in the letters, words, mitzvot, and stories in the Torah. By attuning our lives to the mitzvot and living according to the Torah cycles of time we align ourselves with a Divine rhythm. The weekly cycle of Shabbat, the Jewish calendar in sync with the waxing and waning of the moon, the holidays and their intrinsic connection to the changing seasons, all link us to God's rhythm and Divine plan for creation.

In order to meditate, a person would clear his schedule for a specific period of time, turn off the radio, TV, cell phone, and any other distraction, and clear the mind in order to meditate. This is the secret of all the restrictions of Shabbat, which allow us to free ourselves from the hustle and bustle of the week, affording us the time and the quiet to enter into a more spiritual and meditative state of consciousness. In this sense Shabbat can be related to as a full-day meditation, and all the activities of the day can be approached from a relaxed, peaceful, and sacred mind space. It is no surprise, then, that a favorite activity on Shabbat is singing. Even synagogues that have little or no singing during weekday services incorporate song into the prayers on Shabbat, and the meals are accompanied by joyous group singing. The songs of the third and last meal are usually more meditative and are tinged with a bit of melancholy for the beloved Shabbat which is about to depart. These songs express the great longing of the soul for holiness and for the time that will be "all Shabbat," the Messianic era.

Through pursuing a life of holiness and purity we create proper vessels for God's light and are able to experience Divine Providence. Paradoxically, by living a Torah life with its manifold mitzvot defining almost every area of life we sharpen and clarify our own free will and the ability to act in the world according to our highest ideals and dreams. Music, meditation, prayer, and Torah study ultimately need to merge together and be used to consciously assist us in bringing out our latent potential, so that we can rectify ourselves and accomplish our purpose in this world.

Nature

Another important way of becoming sensitive to our own particular song is spending time in nature, where we experience and hear the song of creation in all its manifold forms: the wind and the rain, a flowing river and crashing ocean waves, wheat rippling in a field and trees swaying in the forest, the humming of insects and the chirping of birds, the cows mooing in the pasture and the wolves howling at night. The more we listen, the more we hear. The more at peace we become, the more the music all around engulfs us and gives over its secrets.

In the vision of the chariot, Ezekiel the prophet describes his vision: "And I looked and behold a storm wind came out of the north, a great cloud and a fire flaring up and a brightness was about it, and out of the midst of it, as it were the color of electrum, out of the midst of the fire" (Ezekiel 1:4). The Hebrew word for "electrum" is *chashmal*, a mysterious word which can be read according to its two syllables — *chash*, meaning "silent," and *mal*, meaning "speaking." The paradox of "speaking silence" applies to the silent music infused in every point of physical matter and at all levels of souls and Divinity.

When Elijah the Prophet escaped to the Sinai Desert, the word of God came to him: "And behold God passed by and a great and strong wind rent the mountains and broke the rocks in pieces before God; but God was not in the wind; and after the wind an earthquake, but God was not in the earthquake; and after the earthquake a fire, but God was not in the fire, and after the fire a still silent voice. And when Elijah heard it he wrapped his face in his mantel and went out and stood in the entrance of the cave" (Kings I 19:11–13). The prophets of old would go to the silence of the desert in order to hear the word of God. The word for desert in Hebrew is *midbar*, which has the same root as "to speak." Through hearing the word of God and aligning it to his own inner song, the prophet gains the strength to speak. Again we are confronted by the paradox of the "speaking silence." Being in nature among God's handiwork sensitizes us to the music of creation, both audible and silent, and awakens within us a great desire to join its song.

Music on Every Level of Existence

Just as prayer is something we are, not what we do, so too music is not something we enjoy or play, but who we are on so many levels. Similar to the idea of the Hebrew letters being the building blocks of creation, music manifests itself at all levels of reality, and we need to become aware of its all-encompassing presence. Music in our lives has the ability to make peace between all the multiplicity we experience, creating a sense of unity and oneness.

Rabbi Avraham Yitzchak Kook, the first chief rabbi of Palestine, wrote a most magnificent description of song:

> There is one who sings the song of his own life, and in himself he finds everything, his full spiritual satisfaction.
>
> There is another who sings the song of his people. He leaves the circle of his own individual self, because he finds it without sufficient breadth, without an idealistic basis. He aspires towards the heights, and he attaches himself with a gentle love to the whole community of Israel. Together with it he sings its songs. He feels grieved in its afflictions and delights in its hopes. He contemplates noble and pure thoughts about its future and probes with love and wisdom its inner spiritual essence.

There is another who reaches toward more distant realms, and he goes beyond the boundary of Israel to sing the song of man. His spirit extends to the wider vistas of the majesty of man generally, and his noble essence. He aspires towards man's general goal and looks forward to his higher perfection. From this source of life he draws the subjects of his meditation and study, his aspirations and his visions.

Then there is one who rises toward wider horizons, until he links himself with all existence, with all God's creatures, with all worlds, and he sings his song with all of them. It is of one such as this that tradition has said that whoever sings a portion of song each day is assured of having a share in the World to Come.

And then there is one who rises with all these songs in one ensemble, and they all join voices. Together they sing their songs with beauty; each one lends vitality and life to the other. They are sounds of joy and gladness, sounds of jubilation and celebration, sounds of ecstasy and holiness.

The song of the self, the song of the people, the song of man, the song of the world all merge in him at all times, in every hour.

And this full comprehension rises to become the song of holiness, the song of God, the song of Israel, in its full strength and beauty, in its full authenticity and greatness. The name Israel stands for *shir Keil*, the song of God. It is a simple song, a twofold song, a threefold song, and a fourfold song. It is the Song of Songs by Solomon, whose name means "peace" or "wholeness." It is the song of the King in whom is wholeness.

(*Orot HaKodesh*, vol. II, p. 444-445)

The mystical power of music and its profound attraction for

the soul reflects the teaching of the Arizal that in essence man is a small world and the world is a big man. The physical and spiritual nature of man incorporates all creation, while all reality is modeled on the secret of man being in the Divine image. Music is manifest in both the microcosm and the macrocosm and it is the very pulse of the universe and life itself. The *Zohar* teaches that God, Torah, and Israel are one (*Zohar* 3:73a). Music and song are the strings upon which this unity is expressed. The blueprint of creation, along with the physical and spiritual laws of the universe, are like the musical score, while each part of creation plays its part. There are times for solo performances and times for singing with the choir, times when we are involved and times when we just sit back and listen.

May we all be blessed to hear the song of creation and integrate it into every fiber of our beings, until we become the music itself. Through this we come to realize our potential and accomplish our purpose in life, expressed through our own unique song. May we always strive to rectify and heal, fulfill and reveal the oneness of God, with the great joy that comes from serving Him. May our efforts be directed to redemption and the sounds of the tenth song, a new song to God, waiting to be revealed, quickly and in our days.

About the Author

Rabbi Avraham Arieh Trugman has been involved in Jewish education for over twenty-five years. As a founding member of Moshav Meor Modiim in 1976, he went on to be director at the Moshav's Center of Jewish Education, which successfully ran programs for over five thousand participants from over twenty-five countries a year. In 1988 he took the position of regional director of NCSY in Denver, Colorado, where he and his wife created a new region. He returned to Israel in 1995 and currently serves as the director of Ohr Chadash: New Horizons in Jewish Experience, which he founded with his wife.

Rabbi Trugman is the author of *Seeds and Sparks: Inspiration and Self-Expression through the Cycles of Jewish Life* (Targum Press, 2003) and has published articles and poems in a wide variety of publications. He appears at Shabbat programs and lectures extensively worldwide.

OHR CHADASH
New Horizons in Jewish Experience

Ohr Chadash is a nonprofit educational organization serving English-speaking students enrolled at various universities, yeshivot, seminaries, and long-term programs in Israel, as well as adults, immigrants, and native Israelis. We provide a wide range of programs in an open, joyous, noncoercive, and spiritual atmosphere, where participants are able to explore Judaism at their own pace. Programs include classes, workshops, lunch and learn, concerts, *Shabbatons*, home hospitality, leadership training, seminars, tours, counseling, and social action projects. We combine heart and mind and cater to each participant's special needs. We provide a home away from home for students and visitors and maintain strong relationships for years to come.

Ohr Chadash has run programs for many thousands of people from the full gamut of Jewish backgrounds. With the inspiration and skills that students gain they return to their home communities eager to take leadership roles. Many students and adults return to Israel and the bonds become even stronger. As educational follow-up, Ohr Chadash runs and participates in events and programs in cities throughout North America.

Rabbi Avraham Arieh and Rachel Trugman, Directors
Moshav Mevo Modiim, D.N. Hamercaz, Israel, 73122
Tel: 972-8-926-5247   Fax: 972-8-926-5448
E-mail: trugman@netvision.net.il